AF269895

the new money strategy

BRANDON VAN DER KOLK

THE MODERN GUIDE TO rational, long-term investing

WILEY

Library of Congress Cataloging-in-Publication Data:

Name: Brandon van der Kolk, author
Title: The new money strategy: the modern guide to rational, long-term
  investing/Brandon van der Kolk.
Description: Hoboken, New Jersey: John Wiley & Sons, Inc, [2026] |
  Includes bibliographical references and index. | Summary: "Investing is
  more accessible than ever, yet increasingly confusing, with trading
  apps, social media influencers, constant market predictions, and endless
  "hot tips" encouraging speculation rather than disciplined wealth
  building. As a result, many investors chase hype, attempt to time the
  market, or feel paralyzed by conflicting advice, leading to volatile
  portfolios, frustration, and a growing sense that financial freedom is
  out of reach. If the market feels overwhelming or stacked against you,
  you are not alone-this common experience is precisely why this book
  exists."—Provided by publisher.
Identifiers: LCCN 2026002116 | ISBN 9781394369843 cloth | ISBN
  9781394432769 paper | ISBN 9781394369867 adobe pdf | ISBN
  9781394369850 epub
Subjects: LCSH: Investments | Stock exchanges | Finance, Personal
Classification: LCC HG4521 .K59 2026
LC record available at https://lccn.loc.gov/2026002116

CONTENTS

CONTENTS

FOREWORD BY PHIL TOWN

Most people think investing is about finding the next hot stock or predicting what will happen in the market tomorrow. They sit glued to CNBC, watching the ticker roll across the screen, convinced that if they can just get the right piece of news faster than the next guy, they will strike it rich. And for a while, maybe it feels like it is working. They get a win or two and think they have cracked the code. But then the tide turns, as it always does, and those gains vanish just as quickly as they appeared. I have seen this story play out countless times.

What most people are doing in the stock market is not really investing at all. It is gambling. The average investor underperforms the market not because they are stupid but because they are playing the wrong game, trying to outguess Wall Street's algorithms and billion-dollar trading firms. That is a battle they will never win.

But there is another way. A better way. The kind of investing that Warren Buffett, Charlie Munger, and my mentor taught me. The strategy is built on patience, discipline, and buying wonderful businesses at wonderful prices. It is not flashy. It does not make headlines. But it works because it is rooted in timeless principles that never change, no matter what new technology or market trend dominates the news cycle.

That is why I am excited about Brandon's book, *The New Money Strategy*. At a time when the noise around investing has never been louder, this book is a steady voice reminding us what real investing actually is. Brandon has studied Buffett, Munger, Graham, and other greats, and more importantly, he has done the hard work of translating their lessons for today's world. Through his New Money YouTube channel, his education company, and now this book, he has taught millions of people how to invest wisely.

What makes Brandon stand out is his gift for simplicity. He can take a concept Wall Street insiders have used for decades and break it down so that anyone, no matter their background, can understand and apply it. That matters because the financial world often hides behind jargon and complication. Brandon cuts through the noise, and this book is his clearest guide yet.

The New Money Strategy blends the best of both worlds: the steady foundation of passive investing with the high-upside potential of Buffett-style stock picking. It is grounded in principles that have stood the test of time but designed for the reality of today's markets. At a moment when investors are being tempted by meme stocks, crypto, and AI hype, Brandon shows a smarter way forward.

I first came across Brandon through his New Money channel and immediately saw he was the real deal. He was not chasing views with flashy predictions; he was teaching the principles I have spent my life sharing, in a way that connected with a new generation. Since then, I have gotten to know him personally, and I can tell you this: he cares deeply about helping people succeed. He is not in this for a quick win or a burst of popularity. He is in it for the long haul, just like the strategy he teaches.

Last year, Brandon and I ran an investing workshop together in Atlanta. I watched him work directly with investors, answering their questions, breaking down complex ideas, and guiding them step by step. It confirmed what I already knew: Brandon is not only a skilled investor; he is also a gifted teacher.

So, when I say you can rely on this book, I mean it. Brandon has done the work, lived the lessons, and proven that he can teach them clearly and effectively. If you give this book your attention, you will walk away with a strategy that is simple to follow, powerful in its results, and grounded in principles that have stood the test of time.

Now it is your turn. Whatever brought you to these pages—frustration with your results, a desire for more control, or just confusion about all the noise around investing—you are in the right place. Do not skim this book. Do not treat it like just another financial read. Work through it. Apply it. Put it into practice in your own investing.

You do not have to gamble in the market. You do not have to hand your money to Wall Street insiders. You can invest wisely, safely, and profitably if you are willing to learn and commit. That is what this book is about. So, turn the page, and let Brandon show you how to take control of your financial future with a strategy that is simple, smart, and built to last.

Phil Town

Three time *New York Times* Best-Selling Author, Hedge Fund Manager, and Founder of Rule #1 Investing

PREFACE

THE PROBLEM

Investing has never been easier to access, and yet for most people, it has never felt more confusing. Anyone can download a trading app in minutes, open a brokerage account, and start buying stocks before lunch. Social media is overflowing with financial influencers, the news cycle is filled with predictions about the next crash or the next boom, and YouTube offers an endless stream of "hot stock tips" and "cannot miss opportunities."

On the surface, this looks like a golden age for investors. But behind the scenes, the reality is very different. More people are investing than ever before, yet many are not building wealth at all. They are speculating. They are chasing hype, buying the latest "sure thing," or trying to time the market based on whatever headline flashes across their screen that day. Others sit frozen, overwhelmed by all the conflicting advice, unable to take the first step.

The result is predictable. Portfolios rise and fall with little rhyme or reason. Excitement turns to frustration. Hope is replaced with regret. And the dream of "financial freedom," the whole reason people wanted to invest in the first place, feels further away than ever.

If you have ever felt like the market is rigged against you, or that you are always one step behind, or that no matter what you do the outcome is out of your control, you are not alone. That is the experience of the average investor today. And it is exactly why this book exists.

WHY A DIFFERENT APPROACH IS NEEDED

At its core, investing is not supposed to be about outguessing the crowd or predicting tomorrow's headlines. It is supposed to be about owning great businesses, holding them over time, and letting compounding work its magic. The problem is that in today's world, that message has been drowned out.

What most people are doing in the stock market is not investing. It is gambling. Buying a stock because someone on Twitter said it was "going to the moon" is not investing. Jumping in and out of crypto coins because a friend swears "they are the future of money" is not investing. Even sitting on the sidelines waiting for the "perfect time" to invest is not investing. All these behaviors are reactive, emotional, and unsustainable.

The truth is that there is a better way. A smarter way. A way that has been proven to work for nearly a century, across bull markets, bear markets, recessions, wars, and every kind of disruption you can imagine. The world's best investors, including Warren Buffett, Charlie Munger, Benjamin Graham, and Peter Lynch, all built their fortunes on timeless principles of patience, rationality, and discipline.

This book is about translating those principles into a clear, practical strategy that anyone can use today. This strategy does not rely on guessing the future or reacting to noise. It is simple, powerful, and sustainable.

PURPOSE OF THIS BOOK

The goal of *The New Money Strategy* is to give you clarity and confidence. My aim is to hand you a playbook that takes the guesswork out of investing and replaces it with a system you can trust.

You will not find gimmicks or shortcuts in these pages. What you will find is a framework that will help you avoid the traps that cause most investors to lose money, and it will put you on a path to building real, lasting wealth.

This is not about making you a finance nerd. It is about making you a rational, long-term investor. If you can follow a few simple steps, and if you have the temperament to stick with them through the ups and downs of the market, you will outperform the vast majority of investors out there.

By the end of this book, you will understand not only how to build a strong investing foundation, but also how to spot wonderful businesses, how to know when to buy and when to hold, and how to avoid the emotional traps that destroy wealth. In other words, you will walk away with a robust strategy that works in all market conditions.

WHO THIS BOOK IS FOR

This book is written for everyday people. You do not need a background in finance. You do not need to be a math genius or a spreadsheet wizard. You do not need to spend hours every day reading financial reports or watching stock tickers.

What you do need is a willingness to learn and the patience to follow through. If you are someone who wants to take control of your financial future, build wealth for yourself and your family, and stop feeling like investing is a gamble, this book is for you.

It does not matter if you are just starting out, or if you have been investing for years but feel like you are spinning your wheels. This strategy works whether you have $500 to invest or $500,000. The principles do not change.

THE FOUR STEPS OF THE NEW MONEY STRATEGY

The strategy outlined in this book is built around four simple steps. Think of them as the four pillars that will support your entire investing journey.

Step 1: Get Prepared

Before you invest a single dollar, you need to make sure your financial foundation is solid. That means clearing high-interest debt, building an emergency fund, ensuring your cash flow is positive, and committing to a long-term mindset. Without this preparation, even great investments can turn into painful losses if life forces you to sell at the wrong time.

Step 2: Lay the Foundation

The next step is to put your wealth creation on autopilot by setting up a passive investing plan. This is the core of your portfolio, built with broad-based index funds or exchange-traded funds (ETFs). It is designed to grow steadily over time with minimal effort on your part and to give you the peace of mind that your financial future is secure no matter what.

Step 3: Find Buffett's Bargains

Once your foundation is in place, you can go on the hunt for extraordinary opportunities. This is where Warren Buffett's playbook comes in: buying wonderful businesses at wonderful prices. You will learn how to identify strong companies with durable competitive advantages, trustworthy management, and attractive valuations. These investments are the ones that can multiply your wealth many times over.

Step 4: Stay the Course

Finally, you need a set of rules to help you stay disciplined. This step is about knowing when to buy, when to sell, and how to hold your investments through thick and thin. It is about setting up circuit breakers that protect you from emotional decisions and keep you focused on the long game.

Together, these four steps form a strategy that is both safe and powerful. They give you the structure to protect your downside, the tools to capture upside, and the discipline to actually see it through.

WHY THIS BOOK IS DIFFERENT

There are plenty of books on investing out there, but most fall into one of two camps. Some tell you to index everything and never touch an individual stock. Others encourage you to chase stock-picking strategies that sound exciting but often lead to unnecessary risk.

This book combines the best of both worlds. It shows you how to build a reliable passive investing foundation that will quietly grow your wealth in the background. At the same time, it gives you the knowledge, tools, and confidence to pursue Buffett-style stock picking in a way that is rational, structured, and low-risk.

What makes this book unique is that it does not ask you to choose between passive and active investing. Instead, it shows you how to use both, side by side, in a way that can supercharge your results.

It is also written for today's world. Let's be real. The financial landscape has changed since Benjamin Graham wrote *The Intelligent Investor* or Peter Lynch wrote *One Up on Wall Street*. We live in a time of social media hype, zero-commission apps, crypto speculation, meme stocks, and constant noise. The principles of great investing have not changed, but the way we apply them must adapt. This book is about bridging that gap.

A WORD OF ENCOURAGEMENT

If all this still feels intimidating, let me leave you with some encouragement. Successful investing is not about being the smartest person in the room. It is not about predicting the next big trend or finding secret information no one else has. It is about patience, discipline, and temperament.

As Warren Buffett often says, "Investing is not a game where the guy with the 160 IQ beats the guy with the 130 IQ." Once you have ordinary intelligence, the real advantage comes from controlling your emotions and sticking to a sound plan.

That is good news because it means anyone can do this. You can do this. If you are willing to learn and commit, you already have everything you need to succeed.

My hope is that as you work through this book, you will begin to see investing not as a gamble or a source of stress, but as one of the most powerful tools you have for shaping your future. You will learn to filter out the noise, focus on what matters, and build a strategy that lasts.

So, let's get started.

AI DISCLOSURE

Portions of this work were developed with the assistance of ChatGPT, created by OpenAI. The tool was used to support idea generation during periods of writer's block, to help organize and refine concepts, suggest alternative structures and phrasing for complex ideas, assist in developing analogies, and improve clarity and conciseness. All AI-assisted material was thoroughly reviewed, edited, and integrated by the author. The final analysis, conclusions, and interpretations represent my views and expertise. I take full responsibility for the content and accuracy of this work.

ABOUT THE AUTHOR

Brandon van der Kolk is the founder of New Money, one of the largest investing education platforms in the world with more than one million subscribers on YouTube. Through his videos and courses at New Money Education, Brandon has helped millions of people build a rational, long-term approach to investing inspired by Warren Buffett's principles.

Brandon regularly collaborates with leading value investors, including Guy Spier of *The Education of a Value Investor*, Steve Eisman of *The Big Short*, and Phil Town of *Rule #1 Investing*, and has co-hosted workshops alongside Phil Town in Atlanta. He is also the co-host of the long-running Young Investors Podcast.

An educator at heart, Brandon specializes in breaking down complex financial ideas into clear, practical lessons that empower everyday investors. *The New Money Strategy* is his first book.

ACKNOWLEDGMENTS

This book wouldn't have been possible without the extraordinary team at Wiley. A heartfelt thank you to Judith Newlin, Sherri-Anne Forde, my literary agent Jill Marsal, and my editors Kelly Talbot and Sheryl Nelson. Thank you to everyone who helped guide this project from idea to print.

I owe enormous gratitude to the thinkers who shaped my approach to investing: Warren Buffett, Charlie Munger, Peter Lynch, Guy Spier, Mohnish Pabrai, Phil Town, and many others. To Phil in particular, thank you for your mentorship over the years.

Thank you to my team at New Money, both past and present: Stephen, JJ, Alex, Ed, Aaron, and Claude for your creativity, work ethic, and unwavering belief in what we're building. And to Natasha, your support, patience, and encouragement kept me going through the long months of writing.

To my family, thank you for the values you instilled in me and for always believing in this journey. And finally, to everyone who's watched, listened, and read New Money over the years—thank you. Your curiosity and passion for learning about investing made this book worth writing.

STEP 0

BEFORE YOU BEGIN

CHAPTER ONE

THE *NEW* MONEY

This book has the potential to drastically change your financial life, just as the ideas within it have changed mine. That's not meant to sound arrogant or self-congratulatory. In fact, very little in these pages is truly original. What you'll find here is a collection of timeless lessons I've absorbed from some of the world's greatest investors over the past decade, wisdom that has turned everyday people—like you and I—into *billionaires*. And the crazy thing? The strategy is dead simple. It doesn't take a finance degree, a 10,000-line spreadsheet, or decades of experience to understand. All it takes is a deep understanding of a few core concepts, and the temperament to follow through in all conditions. I'm not joking when I say that, in just a few hundred pages, you will have learned a more robust stock market investing strategy than Wall Street would ever use.

It's much needed too. Statistics show that young people are finding it harder to get ahead than ever before. House prices are skyrocketing, the stock market seems more volatile than ever, and the safety of term deposits or government bonds will barely keep up with inflation. These days, getting ahead isn't as easy as it used to be. Over the last few years, interest rates have risen to the highest levels we've seen since the turn of the century, inflation has sparked a cost-of-living crisis in many parts of the world, there's political instability, spiraling national debt, global trade tensions, major technological disruption, even war. Everything that could possibly change in our financial world is changing. And where should we be putting our money during all of this? You'd be forgiven for thinking the answer might be "under your mattress."

But what if I told you there is a robust investing strategy that a vast majority of the world's most successful investors use, and it works regardless of what's happening in financial markets? A strategy that world famous investors like Benjamin Graham, Warren Buffett, and Charlie Munger all used to earn billions of dollars? Well luckily, *there is*. And that's exactly what this book will teach you.

The strategy was first created by Benjamin Graham (the grandfather of value investing) and then refined over many decades by his pupil, Warren Buffett. Buffett has long advocated for this strategy and by applying it himself over the past 60 years, he has transformed Berkshire Hathaway from a struggling textile manufacturer in the 1960s into one of the world's largest companies today. Since he took over the company back in 1965, his investment decisions have returned an average of 19.9% per year to Berkshire shareholders, making him *objectively* the World's Best Investor. Sure, many investors have achieved higher returns from year to year, but to have averaged 19.9% for 60 years is something no one has ever done. This high level of compounding sustained for such a long period of time means that if you had invested $1,000 in Berkshire Hathaway shares back in 1965, your shares would be worth a staggering $53 *million* today. How's that for a life-changing investment?

Now, while I can't promise that *The New Money Strategy* will turn $1,000 into $53 million, the strategy outlined in this book is the exact same method that Warren Buffett has preached for more than five decades. Let me be clear, this isn't a get-rich-quick scheme, so you won't find discussions on the latest "meme coin" or trading signals here. Instead, you'll learn a straightforward, time-tested framework for rational long-term investing, the same approach that has been used by the world's greatest investors to build their generational wealth.

OUR FINANCIAL REALITY

Today, *The New Money Strategy* is more crucial than ever, as financial stability becomes increasingly difficult to achieve. As of the time of writing, the median weekly earnings for full-time wage and salary workers is $1,139 (US Bureau of Labor Statistics, 2025), and while that number has grown 21% over the past five years (US Bureau of Labor Statistics, 2020), inflation has outpaced it. The rise in the Consumer Price Index (a common measure of inflation, tracking the price of a basket of everyday goods and services) has clocked in at 22.8% across the past five years (Trading Economics, 2025), which means that, despite wage increases, the average worker's purchasing power has actually declined. The result? Many Americans feel like they're stuck in a financial loop. Savings rates have plummeted, with Americans setting aside just 4.6% of their disposable income today, less than half the 10% savings rate seen in the 1960s and 1970s (Trading Economics, 2025).

It gets even more concerning when you look at retirement savings. According to the Federal Reserve's latest *Survey of Consumer Finances* (2023), nearly half of Americans (46%) have no retirement savings at all (Aladangady et al., 2023). Among those who do, the median

Table 1.1   Holding and Values of Assets of Americans, 2023

Balance sheet item	Percent holding (%)	Conditional median value
Transaction accounts	98.6	$8,000
Certificates of deposit	6.5	$26,000
Savings bonds	6.4	$2,000
Bonds	1.1	$210,400
Stocks	21.0	$15,000
Pooled investment funds	11.5	$150,000
Retirement accounts	54.3	$86,900
Cash value life insurance	16.1	$9,700
Other managed assets	6.2	$140,000
Other	9.4	$6,000

Source: Aladangady et al., 2023

balance across all retirement accounts (including 401(k) plans, IRAs, and thrift savings accounts) is just $87,000.

The reality is, Americans are not saving, which is particularly concerning when you consider our increasing life expectancies thanks to modern medicine. This is true across most of the world, including the United Kingdom. In 2013, a report by the House of Lords noted that for the 2007 birth cohort, 50% of them may still be alive by the time they are 103 (UK House of Lords, 2013). For the young people of today, learning to invest is no longer an exercise in getting rich; it's simply necessary to ensure we'll survive a 30+ year retirement.

Unfortunately, as Table 1.1 shows, the statistics from the Federal Reserve's recent *Survey of Consumer Finances* don't get much better when looking at other investments either. The following was found among survey respondents:

- Fifty-four percent had money saved in retirement accounts (median balance: $87,000)

- Twenty-one percent had savings invested in stocks (median balance: $15,000)
- Twelve percent had investments in pooled funds like mutual funds and REITs (median balance: $150,000)
- Seven percent held Certificates of Deposit (median balance: $26,000)
- One percent owned bonds (median balance: $211,000)

Aladangady et al., 2023

Even in an optimistic scenario, where someone holds the median amount in each of these financial assets (highly unlikely), their total retirement pool would still only be $489,000.

A common rule of thumb in retirement planning is the 4% rule, which suggests that retirees can safely withdraw 4% of their savings per year without depleting their funds too quickly. Well, applying this rule to a $489,000 retirement pool gives just $19,560 per year, hardly enough to cover basic expenses. Even when combined with Social Security, which as of the time of writing, provides an average monthly benefit of $1,976 ($23,712 per year), this would leave a retiree with just $43,272 in retirement income per year (US Social Security Administration, 2025). I don't think I need to convince you that this is a bleak situation. The reality is that we, the young generation, now more than ever, need to be investing for the well-being of our future selves.

A SHORT ROAD TO RUIN

It was by sheer luck that I discovered the world of the stock market, and even more lucky was that I discovered it before my working career even began. If you've followed my content on the New Money YouTube channel for any length of time, you'll know that I am *not* a nerdy finance type. Really, I am just like you. I never had a background in investing. I never studied business or finance. In fact, I studied physical therapy at the University of Canberra in Australia. Back then I was gearing up for a life of rehabilitating the weekend warriors and fixing the sore necks of slumping desk workers. Ignorantly, it was only at the end of my degree that I even bothered looking at my future earning potential, and when I did, I got a very big shock. At the time, all the graduate positions I could find started with a salary of A$60,000 ($38,000 USD) and when I dug deeper, I saw that in the long run, my salary ceiling was likely around A$120,000 ($75,000 USD) unless I owned my own practice or worked for the government in health policy (neither of which I wanted to do).

It was at this point that I realized that these salaries did not match my high-minded ambitions, and thus, 22-year-old Brandon decided he needed to do something about it. I started looking into methods of turning my money into more money and soon came across the world of stock market investing. My eyes lit up. You could buy part ownership in a company like Apple or Tesla and profit from their success? The whole idea blew my mind. Well … that is until I actually started testing it out. Not knowing the faintest thing about rational, long-term stock, I naturally dived in headfirst. I would watch YouTube video after YouTube video discussing which stocks the Australian fund managers were buying. I read article after article on the "hottest stocks on the market." I added Vita Group to my portfolio, then Servcorp, then Healthscope. I was really doing it! I was an investor. Then it all fell apart.

All these stocks suffered steep share price declines, and my hopes and dreams of becoming a stock market millionaire were crushed. One of the companies, Vita Group, collapsed a staggering 72.5% (see Figure 1.1), crushing my spirit. But really, this was exactly what I needed. Although it didn't feel like it at the time, this moment was a huge blessing in disguise. Because it was at that point that I realized

Figure 1.1   Vita group share price.

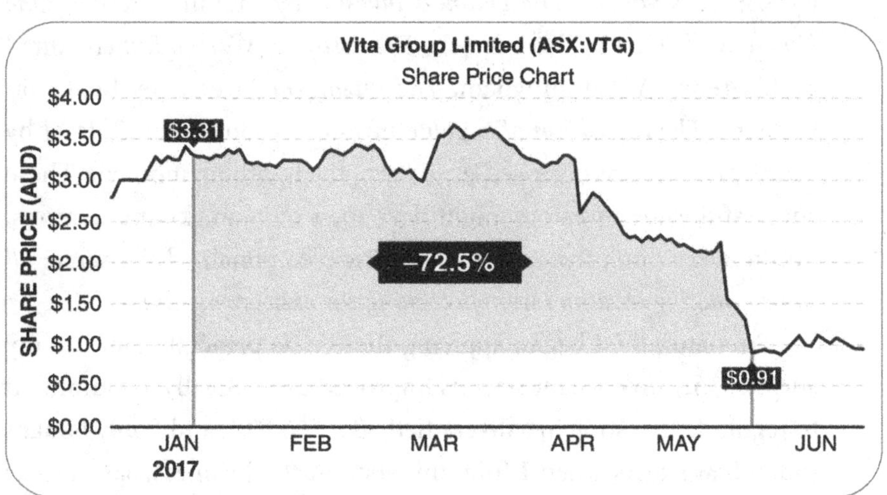

that while the stock market can be a reliable wealth *builder*, it can also be a rapid wealth *killer*. Luckily for me, I didn't have much money to lose back then.

After a series of frustrating losses, I decided to call my Uncle Peter, who has built a very successful career out of helping people make smart long-term investment decisions in the field of retirement planning and Superannuation (Australia's retirement accounts). It was on this phone call that he taught me a word I had clearly never understood before; "diversification" and hinted that if I wanted to try my hand at looking into individual stocks, it might be worthwhile reading a book or two, preferably if they talk about a "Mr. Warren Buffett."

Peter helped me realize something important. If I were to capture the wealth-building potential of the stock market, I needed a robust, proven strategy. At the time I was throwing darts at the board expecting a bullseye, but I was effectively blindfolded. I had no strategy. My strategy was to simply buy what the "smart people" said they were buying, and every single time it ended in disaster.

And so, I read. Book, after book, after book. *Rich Dad, Poor Dad* by Robert Kiyosaki, *The Dhando Investor* by Mohnish Pabrai, *One Up on Wall Street* by Peter Lynch, *The Essays of Warren Buffett* edited by Lawrence A. Cunningham, *The Intelligent Investor* by Benjamin Graham, *The Education of a Value Investor* by Guy Spier, *Rule #1* by Phil Town … I was obsessed. And then, the lightbulb moment. These successful value investors might have their own quirks and nuances, but in every book the underlying principles remained the same: *all these amazing investors were preaching the exact same thing.*

So, naturally, I began applying these new principles, and to my surprise, my investment returns improved dramatically. I committed to regularly investing in a diversified S&P 500 ETF, and I only bought individual stocks when I fully understood the business, saw a clear competitive advantage, had done my digging on the management, and had calculated that it was trading at a margin of safety price.

I couldn't believe it. I was finally *making* money from investing. It felt like I had unlocked the secret to success. And the truth is, I had. It was at that moment that I made what would become one of the most pivotal decisions of my life: I started sharing what I was learning about investing on YouTube.

Fueled by my excitement, I launched the "Aussie Wealth Creation" YouTube channel, using it as a space to document my early mistakes and share the lessons I was learning from world-class investors. At first, I made videos simply because I enjoyed it, it was a way to track my own progress. But as time went on, I realized I wasn't alone. There were millions of people out there, just like me, eager to learn about long-term, Warren Buffett–style investing.

To my surprise, my channel started gaining traction worldwide. By 2020, after surpassing 100,000 subscribers, I rebranded to "New Money," and the rest is history. Fast forward to today, the channel has grown to over a million subscribers, with hundreds of thousands of viewers tuning in each week, and thousands of customers now learning the Warren Buffett way through our video courses on New Money Education (to learn more visit www.newmoney.education).

That's my investing journey in a nutshell, and now I want to show you the secrets I have learned. Because unfortunately, while a lot of young people have woken up to the necessity of investing in recent years, many are walking into the exact same traps I did too: overconfidence, treating the market like a casino, buying into hype without understanding the business. These traps continue to plague new investors, and it's costing them dearly.

THE LESSONS OF ROBINHOOD

Since the COVID-19 pandemic, millions of newcomers have poured into the market through flashy, zero-commission apps. Researchers estimate that roughly 30 million new US retail investors opened brokerage accounts across 2020–2022 (Einhorn et al., 2023), and retail trading climbed to about 25% of total equity volume by 2021 (Public. com, 2023), roughly double a decade earlier.

Robinhood became the symbol of this wave. Powered by stimulus checks, new investors flocked to the stock market, and by mid-2021, Robinhood saw its funded accounts jump to 22.5 million, with 21.3 million monthly active users and more than $100 billion in assets under custody (Robinhood Markets, Inc., 2021). On the surface, this looked like a win. Investing was suddenly accessible to everyone. But in practice, these platforms encouraged behaviors that made markets feel more like casinos than wealth-building machines. Options trading, margin investing, and meme-stock speculation became the norm for many young investors. With flashing graphics, instant notifications, and even "confetti" to celebrate trades, these platforms gamified what should be a serious and disciplined pursuit.

Staggeringly, in 2021, options trading generated about *half* of Robinhood's transaction-based revenue (approximately $689 million out of $1.40 billion). Next up was cryptocurrency at $419 million, and in last place we find equities (stocks), contributing just $288 million (Robinhood Markets, Inc., 2022). The short of it: new investors on Robinhood were running straight toward the highest risk investing strategies, and Robinhood was loving it. These casino-like strategies were making Robinhood billions, and they leaned into it, gamifying the experience. In Massachusetts, the state securities division alleged that about 68% of Robinhood customers in the state who were approved for options reported no or limited investing experience (Massachusetts Securities Division, 2021). By "democratizing investing," unfortunately all these apps did was create a funnel where young people were led straight toward the roulette tables.

The result? Many people who could have set themselves up with a lifetime of steady wealth instead found themselves gambling on volatile stocks, chasing hype, and in some cases losing everything. The most tragic case was that of Alex Kearns, a 20-year-old college student from Naperville, Illinois. In June 2020, he opened the Robinhood app to see his account showing a negative cash balance of about $730,000 tied to options positions. After emailing support multiple times asking for help and receiving only automated replies, he tragically took his own life. The lesson from Alex Kearns is that the casino culture needs to be stopped. The stock market can be a powerful money maker, but it must be approached with the right strategy. Even Warren Buffett has spoken about this at Berkshire Hathaway's recent annual meetings, warning that investing, in his eyes, has never looked so much like gambling. This casino culture is dangerous, and it highlights why discipline and temperament are more important today than ever before.

LESSONS FROM HISTORY

If you zoom out and study the history of financial markets, you'll notice a pattern. It is almost always the gamblers (those chasing quick riches without a sound strategy) who end up fueling the large, panic-ridden market crashes that occur every 5–10 years. And, interestingly, it is those very moments of panic (when speculators are wiped out) that the world's best investors quietly step in and buy big.

Think about the crashes of 1929, 1987, 2000, and 2008. Each time, millions of investors abandoned the market in fear. Panic swept through financial markets, and mass selling caused prices to plummet irrationally. But those who stayed rational, or better yet, those who bought during the chaos, went on to enjoy extraordinary long-term returns. Buffett is the textbook example of this. In 2008, while the global economy was in meltdown and gamblers rushed for the exit, Buffett stepped in, making notable investments in Goldman Sachs, Wells Fargo, General Electric, and, later, Bank of America. As Buffett himself says, "The stock market is designed to transfer money from the active to the patient." The lesson is clear: history rewards the patient, rational investor who sees crashes not as endings, but as opportunities.

That is why I began studying investors like Warren Buffett, Charlie Munger, Peter Lynch, Mohnish Pabrai, Guy Spier, and Phil Town. These are the investors that took advantage of these significant market declines and made millions—and in some cases *billions*. I spent years reading countless books and articles by these investors, watching interviews they had done, and listening to podcasts explaining their strategies. What I learned over that period was that while each investor has their own quirks and nuances, the core principles they follow share remarkable similarities.

Peter Lynch used to say, "You have to know what you own." Charlie Munger would say, "You have to deal with things you're capable of understanding," and Warren Buffett would say, "You must always stay within your circle of competence." And while there's nuance to each, they're all talking about the same core investing pillar of "understanding your investments." Mohnish Pabrai would hunt for opportunities where "heads I win, tails I don't lose much," whereas Charlie Munger would be looking for a "margin of safety," but in reality, they're talking about exactly the same thing.

They each might have liked a different sauce, but at the end of the day, they were all eating burgers. Their playbooks each differed a little in style, but the foundations were the same. What were those shared foundational principles? There were four big ones.

1. **Rational Investing:** Thay all built wealth by sticking to a rational, long-term investing approach and were never enticed into short-term speculation.
2. **The Power of Time:** The key to all of their successes was compounding their money over decades, not months.
3. **Building a Balanced Portfolio:** Many of the world's great investors preach building a core of safe long-term holdings and then building on that with carefully chosen active investments in high-quality businesses.
4. **Investing in What You Understand:** Regardless of the investor, they all invested in businesses they understood very deeply, and this helped them keep a cool head during the natural volatility of markets.

It's these shared philosophies that are at the very core of *The New Money Strategy*. It is a strategy focused on rational thinking, robust and time-tested investing philosophies, and a commitment to long-term wealth building as opposed to short-term speculation.

The strategy can be thought of as all the teachings of the world's best investors condensed into a simple, four-step approach.

- **Step 1, Get Prepared:** Clear your debts, build your safety net, and get your mindset right for the long road ahead.
- **Step 2, Lay the Foundation:** Set up a robust passive investing plan to build the core of your portfolio and put your wealth creation on autopilot.
- **Step 3, Find Buffett's Bargains:** Use Buffett's principles of value investing to find great businesses at bargain prices to snowball your money.
- **Step 4, Stay the Course:** Set up the circuit breakers to help you stick to your plan, review with discipline, and let time do the heavy lifting.

These four pillars are designed specifically to reduce your risk of losses while maximizing your potential for long-term gains. Over the next few hundred pages, I will teach you exactly how the world's best investors became who they are today, and best of all, you will have every financial metric, stress test, and valuation model that they rely on to be able to execute this strategy yourself. No frills, no hype, no "hot stocks," just a comprehensive, time-tested strategy that has, over decades, turned everyday people like you and I into household names.

These investors who have stood the test of time have done so not because they were lucky, or because they had access to secret information, but because they followed this rational framework and stuck with it through every boom and bust. That is exactly what this book is about. So go grab a coffee, find a quiet corner, and let's get started. Your journey toward financial freedom starts now.

STEP 1

GET PREPARED

CHAPTER TWO

REVIEW YOUR FINANCES

When people think about building wealth, they usually think about investing. Buying stocks. Picking winners. Watching their portfolio grow. But the truth is, successful investing doesn't start with the stock market. It starts with getting your financial life in order.

Before you put a single dollar into shares, you need to make sure you're ready for the journey ahead. Why? Because the truth is, investing only works if you can leave your money in the market and give it time to grow. As Warren Buffett says, his Rule 1 of investing is "don't lose money." And one of the fastest ways to lose money is to invest before you're ready.

If you've got credit card debt hanging over your head, if you're living paycheck to paycheck, or if one unexpected expense could derail your investing journey, the reality is you're not ready to invest yet. To start investing you must be in a position where—no matter what happens—you will not be forced into sudden selling. This is essential because, unfortunately, even great investments go through rough patches. In fact, it's quite possible your investments will *fall* in the weeks or months following your decision to buy. But if you're not prepared for that financially, one unexpected household bill could force you to sell your investment, and that's the worst possible outcome. Nothing is more painful than knowing you're onto a winner, yet one of life's inevitable curveballs forces you to sell at a bad time, turning normal market volatility into a permanent loss of capital. That really sucks.

That's the biggest risk for most people. Not that they'll pick the wrong stock, but that they'll be forced to sell a good one at the wrong time.

The world's top investors—Warren Buffett, Charlie Munger, Peter Lynch, Ben Graham, Mohnish Pabrai, and Guy Spier—all understood this. Investing success isn't just about what you buy. It's about having the right habits, mindset, and financial safety net so you can stay the course.

So, before we dive into Buffett's investing strategy, let's go through a simple pre-investing checklist. Some simple steps to take *before* you start building your portfolio. They're not complicated, but trust me when I say, these four preparatory steps can make the world of difference in the long run.

The Four Preparatory Steps

1. Squash that debt—Eliminate high interest loans dragging you down.
2. Cushion your fall—Build an emergency fund to protect you in a pinch.
3. Check your P&L—Ensure the money coming in more than meets the money going out.
4. Focus on the horizon—Think about how long you've got to invest and commit to the long term.

SQUASH THAT DEBT

Debt is a tricky topic. Some investors use it extensively, while others avoid it entirely. For example, if you invest in property, chances are you're using a significant amount of debt, and in many cases, it's helping you generate solid returns. But it's important to understand that not all debt is created equal. There is good debt, and there is bad debt.

Let's say you take out a $500,000 loan to buy an investment property at a 5% interest rate. You're confident you can rent it out for $700 per week. In this case, debt has actually helped you earn an annual profit of $11,400 before expenses and fees. Here's the simple breakdown:

- Interest on $500,000 at 5% per year = $25,000
- Rental income at $700 per week = $36,400
- Net gain = $11,400 per year

Of course, this doesn't include costs like maintenance, insurance, or taxes, but it illustrates how using debt can be a powerful tool when applied to productive investments. This is what most people refer to as "good debt." "Good debt" is low to moderate interest borrowing that is used to buy assets that generate income or increase in value.

"Bad debt," on the other hand, is a completely different story. This refers to moderate to high interest borrowing used to fund lifestyle expenses. Think credit cards, payday loans, personal loans, unnecessary car loans, and "buy now, pay later" schemes. These debts don't help you build wealth. They quietly drain it.

Financing a modest, reliable car at a low interest rate is not what I'm talking about here. Bad debt in this case refers to borrowing to buy a luxury vehicle you don't need and can't afford.

Table 2.1   Brandon's Unchecked Credit Card Debt

	Debt Outstanding	Annual Interest (at 23.99% p.a.)
Year 1	**$1,000.00**	$239.90
Year 2	$1,239.90	$297.45
Year 3	$1,537.35	$368.81
Year 4	$1,906.16	$457.29
Year 5	$2,363.45	$566.99
Year 6	$2,930.44	$703.01
Year 7	$3,633.46	$871.67
Year 8	$4,505.12	**$1,080.78**

"Bad debt" often comes with interest rates above 10%, which can quickly spiral out of control if left unchecked. Take my own credit card, for example. It has an annual interest rate of 23.99%. Table 2.1 shows what happens if I were to carry a $1,000 balance and leave it unpaid for eight years.

By year 5, my total debt has more than doubled. By year eight the annual interest alone exceeds my original $1000 balance. This is the hidden danger of compound interest. While compound interest can snowball your wealth in the stock market, it can just as easily snowball your debts in the opposite direction. The higher the interest rate, the more vicious the spiral becomes. This is exactly how people find themselves financially crippled by credit card debt, which often carries interest rates above 20% per year.

So why should you focus on paying off high-interest debt before investing?

Let's consider a simple example. Imagine I have $1,000 in savings. I can either invest it in the stock market or use it to pay off a $1,000 credit card balance.

Situation 1: I pay off the debt

At 23.99% interest, my credit card will cost me $239.90 in interest over the next 12 months. By using my $1,000 to eliminate the debt,

I've effectively earned a guaranteed return of 23.99%, simply by avoiding that painful interest cost. I don't walk away with a profit, but at least I'm no longer going backward.

Situation 2: I invest instead

Let's say I invest the $1,000 and manage to earn the historical average return of the S&P 500, which is 10.26% per year. After 12 months, my investment grows to $1,102.60, giving me a profit of $102.60.

But the problem here is that I still have that $1,000 credit card debt. This costs me $269.77 in interest over the same period. So, while my investment made me $102.60, my debt cost me nearly three times as much.

My Net Position

My net position?

Investment return: +$102.60

Interest on debt: −$239.90

Net result: −$137.30

In the first scenario, I break even. In the second, I'm worse off, even though my investment performed well. This is why smart investors always tackle high-interest debt before putting money into the market. Yes, you *might* outperform your debt's interest rate, but the odds are against you. Paying it off first is the more reliable and rational path forward.

What About My Mortgage?

A common dilemma for investors is deciding whether to pay down their mortgage or invest in the stock market. I don't like to sit on the fence, but in this case, the answer really does depend on the individual.

Mortgage debt is not considered "bad debt." While interest rates on home loans can fluctuate, they rarely climb above 10%, which is generally where most people start to classify debt as "high interest." At the time of writing, my own variable mortgage rate is around 6%.

So, what should I do with extra savings? There are two main options:

Option 1: Invest in the stock market

Historically, the S&P 500 has returned around 10% per year (at least it has done since 1957). If we knew with certainty that those returns would continue, then choosing the stock market over your mortgage would be a no-brainer. But unfortunately, markets are unpredictable. There's no guarantee of a 10% return every year, and along the way there will be volatility.

Option 2: Pay down the mortgage

Paying off part of your mortgage gives you something that stock market investing can't: a guaranteed return. If your interest rate is 6%, then every dollar you repay early is effectively earning you a 6% return by eliminating that cost.

So, the question becomes simple: at your current mortgage rate, would you rather lock in a guaranteed return, or chase a potentially higher, but uncertain, return in the market?

The closer your mortgage rate is to 10%, the stronger the case for paying it down. The closer it is to zero, the more sense it makes to invest instead. Either way, there's no wrong answer here. Whether you invest or pay off your home loan, you're improving your financial position. So, choose the option that gives you the most peace of mind and fits your long-term goals.

CUSHION YOUR FALL

Once you've cleared your high-interest debt, the next step is to build an emergency fund. This is a stash of cash set aside for when life throws you a major curveball. Think vet bills, a job loss, a medical emergency, or needing to travel to support a sick family member. These events are unpredictable, often stressful, and usually expensive. The purpose of an emergency fund is to give you financial breathing room, so you're not forced to dip into your investments when something unexpected happens.

This is especially important if you plan to invest in the stock market. In the market, short-term drops are common, and there will be times when your portfolio is down even if your investments are solid. In those moments, the worst thing that can happen is being forced to sell. Remember that with investing, you haven't actually lost money until you lock in the sale, which is why having a financial cushion is so important. Without it, even a small emergency can force you to cash out at the worst possible time, and as we discussed before, that's the real danger of investing without a safety net.

Picture this. After weeks of research, you find a company that ticks every box. Sales are soaring, management is excellent, and the future looks bright. On top of that, a recent production issue at the manufacturing plant has caused the stock to fall below its intrinsic value. You see the opportunity and invest $10,000.

A few days later, the company announces it will take three months to fix the issue. You still feel confident in the long-term prospects, but the market reacts badly, and the share price drops another 50%. Your $10,000 is now worth $5,000. You re-run your numbers and believe the stock could still quadruple from here, but then, life throws a curveball. While you're looking over your outstanding electricity bill, your partner calls. The dog needs emergency surgery, and the vet bill is $4,000.

You have no choice. You don't have the cash to cover the unexpected bill, so you're forced to sell your investment. Not only have you locked in a 50% loss, but you've also lost out on a potential long-term winner.

All of this could have been avoided with an emergency fund. If you had one, you could have covered the vet bill without touching your portfolio.

So, how much should you save? It depends on your situation. A common rule of thumb is to aim for three to six months of living expenses. If your income is unstable or unpredictable, it's safer to aim for six months. If your job is steady and your spending is consistent, three months may be enough.

There is no perfect number. The goal is to simply create a buffer that protects your investments and gives you peace of mind when the unexpected happens. Take the example of two very different life situations, shown in Figure 2.1.

These are two very different financial pictures. Situation 1 involves a casual worker with variable income and expenses, while Situation 2 involves a homeowner with stable income and no mortgage. Despite their weekly expenses being fairly similar, the person in Situation 1 faces more uncertainty and would be wise to aim for a larger emergency fund—closer to six months of expenses, or around $18,000.

By contrast, the person in Situation 2 has steady income, fewer financial obligations, and less variability in their spending. In this case, a three-month emergency fund would likely be enough, which comes to roughly $8,500.

There's no universal number. The right emergency fund is the one that reflects your life, your job security, and how much breathing room you need when things go wrong. The main takeaway is to make

Figure 2.1   The gym worker and the bank manager.

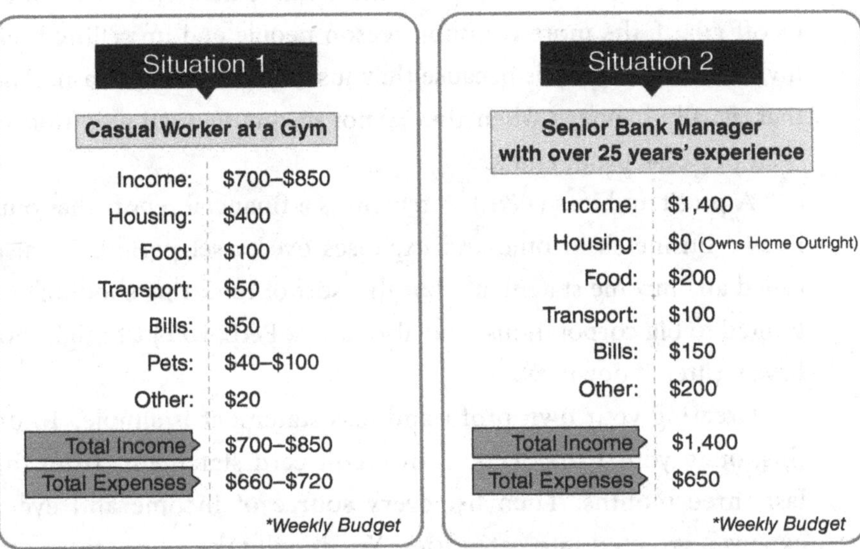

sure you build one up, then lock it away. Remember that to be a successful investor you must be able to leave your money invested in the market, undisturbed for decades.

CHECK YOUR PROFIT AND LOSS

Before you begin investing, another critical preparatory step is to understand your cash inflows and outflows. Yes, I too find budgeting exceptionally dull, but the reality is before you put any money to work in the market, you need to ensure you have more than enough income to comfortably cover your ongoing living expenses. As we've discussed in the preceding paragraphs, the money we invest should remain untouched for as long as possible, and to let compounding do its work, we need to avoid situations where you're forced to pull money out of your investments. And while emergencies can catch us off guard, the more common reason people end up selling their investments abruptly is because they just run too low on cash. And that usually happens when they're not paying enough attention to their personal profit and loss.

A profit and loss (P&L) statement is a financial report that outlines a business's income and expenses over a set period. It's also called an "income statement," but this sort of reporting shouldn't be limited to big corporations. You also have a P&L; you just might not have written it down yet.

Creating your own profit and loss statement is simple. To do this, open your bank account or credit card statements from the last three months. Then list every source of income and every expense, grouped into categories. Yes, it will take a little time and effort, but I guarantee you'll feel more in control of your finances once it's done.

Figure 2.2 shows a simple template you can follow.

Hopefully, after completing that exercise, you've ended up with positive net income. In accounting terms, net income is simply your total income minus your total expenses over a set period. Just like a business, your goal is to ensure your personal P&L generates a healthy profit. That profit is what you can use to invest.

If your net income is zero, or worse, negative, then your first priority should be to increase your income or reduce your expenses. This must be corrected before even considering investing in the stock market. As we've discussed, investing money you can't afford to spare is a quick-fire way to get crushed. I don't recommend it.

Once you've calculated your personal profit over the past three months (and it's healthily in the black), the next step is to

Figure 2.2   Your personal P&L.

Profit and Loss

For the three months ending: _______________________

Income

Primary Income Source: $				
Secondary Income Streams: $	$	$	$	
Dividends & Investment Income: $	$	$	$	

Expenses

Housing: $	$	$	$	$

(mortgage repayments inc. interest, rent, insurances, maintenance)

Transport: $	$	$	$	$

(car payments, gas, maintenance, insurances, public transport, registration fees, parking)

Food & Drink: $	$	$	$	$

(groceries, take out, food subscriptions, alcohol)

Personal: $	$	$	$	$

(streaming services, health + fitness, haircuts, leisure activities)

Pets: $	$	$	$	$

(pet food, insurance, vet bills, accessories)

Utilities: $	$	$	$	$

(water, electricity, gas, internet, phone bill)

Clothing: $	$	$	$	$

(clothes, shoes, accessories, cosmetics)

Medical: $	$	$	$	$

(insurance, dental, doctor, medications, devices)

Financial: $	$	$	$	$

(student loans, accounting, credit card, personal loans, financial planning)

Other: $	$	$	$	$

(gifts, charity, special event, etc.)

Net Income (personal profit) $

decide how much of that surplus you are willing to set aside for investing. While money invested in the market is not literally locked away, as we've discussed it certainly helps to think of it as untouchable. As Warren Buffett says, "Don't buy something for 10 minutes unless you're willing to hold it for 10 years." Adopting the mindset that your investments will be off-limits for the next decade is a helpful way to avoid dipping into them during short-term challenges.

So how much should you invest? That depends on your personal situation. One thing I will say, however, is that it should not be your total "net income." While I'm all for investing aggressively early on, you do not want to invest so much that you are ever left struggling to cover your day-to-day costs. I find that usually leads people to abandon the idea of investing altogether, which doesn't help anything. So, no, don't invest 100% of your net income. But could you set aside, say, 40% of it? What about 60%?

Again, there is no perfect number. Personally, I am still young, living near my family, and have no children. This gives me the freedom to invest 80% or more of my personal profit. On the other hand, a couple with a large home loan, children to care for, and a school trip coming up might only feel comfortable investing 20–30%. And that is completely okay. Personal finance is personal, and it should reflect your life and your comfort level.

Once you've decided on a percentage, the final step is to make the investing process as simple and consistent as possible by *automating* it. We'll dive deeper into this in a later chapter, but for now, the key is to set up a recurring transfer from your bank account to your brokerage account. This takes the decision-making away and keeps you on track with your investing without needing to think about it. The easier you make the system, the more likely you are to stick with it.

FOCUS ON THE HORIZON

As much as I would like it to be, unfortunately, the stock market is not a get-rich-quick scheme. At best, it's a get-rich-slowly strategy. As Warren Buffett famously said, "The stock market is designed to transfer money from the active to the patient." In the world of successful investing, long-term thinking isn't optional; it's essential. With that in mind, the final step in our pre-investing checklist is to decide on your investment time horizon. How long do you plan on committing to this investing thing? While this step may sound vague, it is one of the most important. In fact, it's often where investors trip up the most.

The reality is, we need to commit to investing for the long term. Unlike property, which can take months to buy or sell, shares can change hands in seconds, and it's this speed of trading that makes the market highly volatile in the short run. In the short term, share price fluctuations represent nothing but the market's mood. When investors are excited, prices soar. When they're scared, prices crash. The truth is that short-term price movements often have little to do with the underlying performance of the business. That's why the results of Buffett-style value investing vary so much across the short term. But in the long run, we shine. Why? Because over time, business results matter more than the market's emotions. As Benjamin Graham (Warren Buffett's mentor and author of *The Intelligent Investor*) once famously said, "In the short term the stock market is a voting machine, but in the long run it is a *weighing machine* [emphasis added]." This means that in the long run, the weight of strong business performance can't be overcome by the market's moods.

Take Apple, for example. By the end of December 2007, Apple's stock had already risen more than sevenfold since the start of the decade. The company had strong economics, a great management team, and had just launched the iPhone, a revolutionary product that would change the world. Then the global financial crisis hit.

Despite Apple's strong fundamentals, its share price dropped 61% in just over a year, closing at $2.79 (split-adjusted) in January 2009. That fall had nothing to do with the company's performance. It was simply the result of panic in the broader market. If you had invested $10,000 in Apple on December 27, 2007, you would have been absolutely correct in your analysis of the business, but by the next year, your portfolio would have been down more than $6,000.

That's the risk of short-term investing.

But imagine you had approached that investment with a 10-year mindset. Despite the crash, by 2017 your $10,000 would have grown to $59,387. And if you held all the way through to today, your investment would be worth over $270,000. Pretty cool, right? That's the power of long-term thinking. The strategy is simple: buy great businesses at fair prices and then *give them time to grow*. Without patience, this strategy simply doesn't work.

There's an old saying in investing: "The market can stay irrational longer than you can stay solvent." Now, it's usually used to warn against "shorting" stocks (betting on the share price falling), but the broader message is clear: markets can behave irrationally for far longer than we expect. And I've seen it myself.

Throughout much of the 2010s, the market was fueled by record-low interest rates. Stocks kept climbing, even as many broad market valuation metrics suggested it was getting expensive. Experts warned of an imminent crash. Headlines said the bubble would burst. But it didn't. Year after year, the market rose. It wasn't until the black swan event of COVID-19 that the crash finally came.

Imagine you had listened to all that fear in 2015 and stayed out of the market. Back then, the S&P 500 was around 2,100 points. Five years later, it had climbed to 3,200, a gain of 52%. And amazingly, even after the 34% COVID-19 crash in 2020, your portfolio still wouldn't have been in the red if you had simply stayed invested.

The lesson is simple. In the short term, markets bounce around and often make no sense. Prices move based on headlines, emotions, and short-lived narratives. Trying to predict or time those moves is like swimming against a rip current: it wears you out and gets you nowhere. But over the long run, business performance rises to the top.

Here's another way to think about it. When you look at the wealthiest investors of today, what do you notice? There's something they all have in common ... they're really old! They're wealthy because they've not only held quality investments but have held them for decades to let compounding do the heavy lifting. As Warren Buffett says, someone is sitting in the shade today because someone planted a tree a long time ago.

That's why you need to get clear on your time horizon. Are you planning to invest for a year and hope you strike gold? If that's your mindset, the stock market probably isn't the right place for you. Are you within 10 years of retirement? If so, more stable fixed-income assets like government bonds may be a better fit.

But if you're relatively young, with decades ahead of you and a desire to build real wealth, this book is for you. Over the next few chapters, we'll plant your seed. A seed that, given enough time, will become a beautiful tree to provide shade for you and your family for generations to come.

Getting your finances in order ahead of time might not be flashy, but it could just be the smartest first move you ever make as an investor. By clearing high-interest debt, building an emergency fund, understanding your cash flow, and committing to the long game, you're setting yourself up to play offense, not defense. As Buffett would remind us, his rule number one of investing is "don't lose money." And these four steps are how you set yourself up so that nothing knocks you off track.

But here's the thing: the financial preparation we've discussed in this chapter is only half the story.

Once you've cleared your debts, built your emergency fund, understood your cash flow, and committed to a long-term horizon, the real battle begins. And it does not happen on Wall Street. It happens inside your own mind.

After studying the world's greatest investors, I've come to the realization that successful investing is about 10% brains and 90% temperament. Sadly, I've watched smart people with solid plans fall apart because they could not master their emotions: fear, greed, doubt, impatience. In my experience, these are the true threats to your wealth, and learning to control them is the reason Uncle Warren has outperformed the crowd for so many decades.

Buffett has previously stated he was "wired at birth to allocate capital," not to boast, but to highlight that his edge comes from never letting emotions dictate decisions. As he famously put it: "Investing is not a game where the guy with the 160 IQ beats the guy with the 130 IQ. Once you have ordinary intelligence, what you need is the temperament to control the urges that get other people into trouble in investing."

Charlie Munger was even more blunt: "A lot of people with high IQs are terrible investors because they've got terrible temperaments."

So, before we dive into building the foundation of your portfolio, there is one final step to "get prepared." We need to talk about how to *think* like a world-class investor.

CHAPTER THREE

THE PSYCHOLOGY OF INVESTING

To invest successfully, you don't need a stratospheric IQ, unusual business insights, or inside information. What's needed is a sound intellectual framework for making decisions and the ability to keep emotions from corroding that framework.
— Warren Buffett, foreword to Benjamin Graham's
The Intelligent Investor

When people think of successful investing, they often imagine something very technical: spreadsheets, multiple computer screens, insider connections, or a genius-level IQ. But the truth is, most of the mistakes that investors make have nothing to do with logic, and everything to do with emotion.

Fear. Greed. Doubt. Impatience.

These are the real drivers behind market crashes, poor timing, and portfolio blow-ups. It's not that investors don't know what to do. As we'll discuss later, finding wonderful businesses to invest in is not actually that difficult, and every investor knows the basic "buy low, sell high." The unfortunate thing is that most of the time it's the investors' own emotional reactions that doom them to a lifetime of underperformance.

This chapter is about that emotional control: what it is, why it matters, and importantly, how to develop it. We're going to unpack why emotional discipline consistently outperforms raw intelligence and how mastering your own psychology can be the single greatest edge you bring to the market.

WALL STREET'S BIGGEST LIE

When most people first encounter the stock market, they assume it's a game reserved for the exceptional talent. After all, Wall Street is filled with Ivy League graduates, complex financial models, and hedge fund prodigies. It's easy to believe you need to outsmart everyone else to succeed.

I used to think that too. I thought investing returns came down to who ran the best spreadsheets, had the best degree, and curated the best inside connections. That's why I foolishly began picking stocks based on what I saw the super genius fund managers doing on YouTube. But that belief quickly unraveled as I studied the world's best investors.

Warren Buffett, for example (literally the greatest investor of our time), has *never* claimed to be the smartest guy in the room. As previously stated, Buffett frequently says, "Investing is not a game where the guy with the 160 IQ beats the guy with the 130 IQ." Past a certain point, intelligence doesn't help much. In some cases, it can even be a hindrance if it leads to overconfidence.

What really matters is how you think and how you behave.

Buffett calls it "the investing temperament." It's the ability to stay calm when markets crash, to resist hype when the crowd is euphoric, to hold onto a great business even when everyone else is panicking. This is something he and Charlie Munger were both exceptional at. Over the course of their careers, they saw the quoted value of their Berkshire Hathaway shares (representing almost their entire net worth) plummet by 50% on three separate occasions. But did they panic and sell out? Never. They understood that the price fluctuation was emotional, but the underlying business performance was strong. So, they held on. Today, Berkshire's share price sits close to all-time highs as the business continues to grow steadily over time.

Warren and Charlie had it figured out, and even in my own investing journey, the biggest mistakes I've made weren't the result of poor analysis; they were emotional lapses. One example still stings.

When I was about 20, I made an early investment in Tesla. At the time, I was obsessed with the company. I would spend hours in the Tesla online design studio, customizing endless combinations of the Model S and Model X. I knew every color, wheel, and trim option. I tracked their production numbers, their factory locations, their international delivery logistics. I knew about the upcoming Model 3 ramp-up and the long-term vision for gigafactories in China and Europe. I genuinely believed Tesla could change the world, and I wanted to be a part of it.

So, I invested $10,000. At the time that was a huge amount for me. I was working as a Les Mills fitness instructor, earning about $400 a week, not exactly what you'd call a healthy salary. This $10,000 investment was a big chunk of my net worth, but I had strong conviction and went in with a long-term mindset.

I remembered Buffett's line: "Don't hold a stock for 10 minutes unless you're willing to hold it for 10 years." And I meant it.

Then … the Model 3 delays hit. Short sellers piled on. Headlines turned sour. And despite still believing in the business, I sold half my position. I was spooked by the noise. Over time, that one decision, based on emotion rather than analysis, has cost me approximately $50,000 (and counting). Ouch.

Since then, I've never forgotten the lesson: your temperament will make or break you.

So, if you've ever doubted whether you're smart enough to be a great investor: good news. Remember, you don't need a finance degree or a genius-level IQ. What you need is emotional discipline, patience, and the courage to stick to your convictions when everyone else is panicking.

THE CURRENT EMOTIONAL ENVIRONMENT

In the past, the hardest part of investing was often finding information: company reports, earnings updates, market data. Believe it or not, it used to be difficult to get your hands on these things. Today, it's the opposite. We are drowning in information. The challenge isn't accessing information; it's filtering it out. And more than that, it's resisting the emotional triggers built into the way modern information is delivered.

This is the environment today's investor must navigate. One where every notification, tweet, and headline is designed to provoke a reaction, not support thoughtful decision-making.

Over the last six years, a whole new generation of investors (many inspired by the pandemic-era stock market surge) has entered the game through platforms like Robinhood, eToro, and other commission-free brokers. This accessibility is a double-edged sword. On the one hand, it's empowering more people than ever to build wealth through the stock market. On the other, it has given rise to a new form of gambling culture that has, unfortunately, blurred the line between investing and speculation.

Instead of building conviction over months or years, for these "investors," decisions are made in seconds. A tweet goes viral. A stock spikes. A meme is born. These people buy in, not because they understand the business, but because everyone else seems to be getting rich off it.

Investing has become gamified with confetti animations, swipeable trade screens, and real-time charts mimicking the feedback loops of social media. The experience is fast, exciting, and addictive. But it is not designed to reward long-term thinking. It's designed to keep you glued to your screen, trading stocks, because ultimately, that's how these brokers make their money.

Similarly, social media has also become a double-edged sword. Don't get me wrong, it has opened up some truly fantastic educational channels for investors, but equally, it has also created a culture of hype over substance. On platforms like TikTok and Instagram, the most viral finance content often promotes the worst habits: gambling on penny stocks, YOLOing options trades, and chasing speculative assets with zero understanding of the underlying business.

Instead of learning to value companies, content creators are being taught to trade attention. The more exciting or outrageous the claim, the more engagement it gets. And this creates a false sense of confidence for all involved, because when everyone is suddenly agreeing with you in the comments, the positive feedback loop makes it's easy to think you must be right.

But these echo chambers are dangerous. They amplify our psychological biases, suppress contrarian thinking, and reinforce emotional investing, all of which lead people away from rational, long-term decision-making. At the same time, they hotwire our brains for short-term gratification, with every scroll, like, and click delivering a fresh hit of dopamine. This trains us to crave immediacy: fast wins, quick returns, instant validation.

The truth is that this kind of "investing" is no different from placing chips on a roulette table. It's pure speculation, not grounded in fundamentals, and if you keep doing it over the long run, it almost guarantees failure. Real investing—the one that Uncle Warren teaches—is the exact opposite.

It requires patience, restraint, and often doing nothing for long stretches of time. That's hard to reconcile when the rest of your life is being lived in five-second clips. The platforms we use the most are conditioning us *against* the very qualities that make successful investing possible.

And when you start linking your portfolio to your emotions, feeling euphoric when a stock rises or anxious when it dips, you stop thinking like a business owner and start acting like a gambler. It becomes less about long-term wealth creation and more about short-term excitement, a dangerous trap for any investor.

MEDIA SENSATIONALISM AND THE DEATH OF THOUGHTFUL ANALYSIS

It's not just social media. Traditional financial media is guilty too. Most headlines you see today are engineered for clicks, not clarity. Stories are framed to stir emotion: "These 3 Stocks Could Skyrocket on Earnings," "Is the Market About to Crash?," "Top 10 AI Stocks That Will Make You Rich."

This creates a constant sense of urgency, a feeling that if you're not making a move right now, you're falling behind. It encourages action for action's sake rather than thoughtful, strategic investing.

The reality is the best investors do remarkably little. Warren Buffett once joked that he could improve most portfolios simply by turning off people's internet browsers. Why? Because the more you react to headlines and market noise, the more you're drawn into playing a short-term game in a long-term arena. This is also the reason why Buffett has kept the headquarters of Berkshire Hathaway (one of the largest companies in the world) in the quiet town of Omaha, Nebraska, as opposed to moving it to the hustle and bustle of New York City. In one of his early interviews, he said, "If I were on Wall Street, I'd probably be a lot poorer. You get overstimulated on Wall Street, and you hear a lot of things. In Omaha, you can just sit and think. It's very important to sit and think." By removing himself from the noise, it gives Warren the space he needs to keep a clear head, ensuring the decisions he makes are ones based on logic and reasoning, not based on short-term emotion.

While you might score the occasional quick win by speculating on a meme stock or buying the latest crypto coin, over time, that kind of reactive investing almost always leads to poor results. One of Warren Buffett's most memorable analogies is the "punch card" approach to investing. He suggests imagining you're given a punch card with just 20 slots, and every time you make an investment, one of those slots is used. That's it. Once all 20 are punched, your investing career is over. No take-backs, no do-overs. Just those 20 decisions to build your entire portfolio for life.

It's a simple idea, but it carries a powerful message: if you knew you could only make 20 investments in your lifetime, you'd think very differently about each one. You'd slow down. You'd do more research. You'd ignore market noise and wait patiently for the rare opportunities that truly deserve your capital. You wouldn't chase hype, gamble on speculation, or trade out of boredom. You'd swing only at the fat pitches.

That's the exact philosophy Warren Buffett has followed throughout his investing career, and it's helped him achieve an extraordinary 20% average annual return since 1965. Now, you might assume that kind of performance requires constant buying and selling, but the truth is quite the opposite. In his 2022 annual shareholder letter, Buffett wrote, "Our satisfactory results have been the product of about a dozen truly good decisions—that would be about one every five years" (Buffett, 2023).

In other words, Buffett's success hasn't come from frantic trading or flashy stock picks, it's come from a few big, well-timed bets made with patience and conviction.

The reality of *successful* investing doesn't look like the high-octane fund manager shouting on CNBC, making 20 trades a day in front of a wall of monitors. More often, it looks like someone quietly sitting on their hands, waiting. The real superstars are rarely the loudest. They're the ones thinking long term, acting rationally, and making calm, deliberate decisions, often when everyone else is losing their head.

THE SIX KILLERS OF WEALTH

Of course, while staying patient and rational sounds easy in theory, actually doing it is another story. The truth is, we're all vulnerable to emotional decision-making, especially in high-stakes environments like investing. It's just part of being human. Even when we know what we should do, our brains often push us in the opposite direction. Why? Because we're wired with psychological biases, mental shortcuts that once helped us survive in the wild, but now sabotage our decisions in modern, complex systems like the stock market.

These psychological biases are exactly what traditional media, social media personalities, and even door-to-door salespeople try to exploit. Often without you realizing it, they prey on your subconscious tendencies to keep you on the hook. This has been happening for centuries, and it will continue for centuries to come.

The fact of the matter is we are all vulnerable to these biases because we are human. But there is one powerful way to stop them from influencing your decision-making: understanding what they are and how they work.

While there are *many* behavioral biases out there, we will focus on six in particular that commonly influence investors. Let's go through each.

Confirmation Bias

This is the tendency to subconsciously seek out information that supports what you already believe, while ignoring or dismissing information that contradicts it. As an investor, this often shows up when you own a stock and naturally gravitate toward bullish takes on it (YouTube videos, Reddit threads, articles that praise the company's future), while conveniently skipping over bearish perspectives.

Example

You buy shares in a company with a compelling product. But when earnings start to slow due to a reduction in sales, instead of reassessing your thesis, you double down, believing only the most optimistic analyst notes, and telling yourself it's just a temporary setback. Your subconscious doesn't want to be wrong, so without knowing it you start to filter out any information that might suggest you are.

Overconfidence Bias

This is when you overestimate your knowledge, skill, or ability to predict the future. It's especially common among newer investors who may have experienced a few early wins and start to believe they have a special edge. This bias has become particularly prevalent in young investors over the past six years, riding the wave of upward market momentum and falsely attributing their success to superior skill.

> **Example**
>
> You buy into a few tech stocks like Meta, Microsoft, and Tesla, and thanks to general buying pressure among institutional investors in the tech sector, their share prices rocket up, making you a quick profit. You sell out of your position for a gain, and next week see that these stocks have corrected slightly, falling around 10%. You falsely attribute your exceptional timing to skill, not luck, and filled with confidence, you start making larger bets, trading options, or leveraging up, only to get wiped out completely when the market inevitably turns.

Anchoring Bias

This occurs when we fixate on a specific number or reference point (often the price we bought a stock at) and use it as an anchor for our future decisions, even if the number is no longer relevant. Anchoring is dangerous because it locks you to the past, when successful investing requires assessing the present and making decisions based on today's reality.

> **Example**
>
> You see a stock fall from $150 to $80 and tell yourself, *"It's a bargain; it used to be $150!"* But that $150 price might have reflected unrealistic expectations. Anchoring to that old price may be blinding you to the company's new reality: potentially one of declining earnings, worsening fundamentals, or a changed competitive landscape.

Herding Behavior

Humans are social creatures, and we take comfort in doing what everyone else is doing, especially when the stakes are high. The herding bias is when you follow the crowd simply because you are afraid of being the odd one out. And unfortunately, in investing, that usually means buying high and selling low.

> **Example**
>
> During the GameStop and AMC short squeezes in early 2021, millions of retail investors jumped in, not because they understood the businesses, but because it felt like everyone else was making money. Prices were soaring, and FOMO kicked in. Unfortunately, many who followed the herd near the top got caught holding the bag, suffering losses of up to 85%.

Sunk Cost Fallacy

This is the tendency to hold onto a losing investment simply because you have already committed money, time, or emotional energy to it. Instead of reassessing the situation objectively, you convince yourself,

"I can't sell now, I've already lost too much." For investors, this can be especially dangerous. Sometimes a steep decline in a company's share price signals real, fundamental problems. In those cases, the best decision is often to cut your losses and move on.

Example

You buy a stock at $100, and it soon drops to $60. You know the fundamentals have deteriorated, but instead of reassessing and selling, you close your eyes and hold on, hoping it will rebound. Deep down you know that selling now would mean admitting you made a mistake, and you can't bring yourself to face that reality. Over the next three months the stock falls again, this time from $60 to $40, and you take another 33% loss that could have been avoided.

Recency Bias

Recency bias is when we give too much weight to recent events and trends, assuming they will continue indefinitely, whether it's a declining stock, a market rally, or perhaps a string of positive earnings reports.

Example

After watching tech stocks surge for the last 12 months, you start believing that "tech always wins." You overweight your portfolio, ignoring stretched valuations, and when sentiment shifts, you are caught off guard as the sector corrects. Or, alternatively, the opposite may be happening. You might see a great business decline for months, but with negative headlines dominating, you convince yourself the company will only keep falling. In doing so, you miss out on a prime buying opportunity.

Overcoming Bias

At this point I want to reaffirm that these biases are completely natural, and they affect every one of us. Me, you, even Warren Buffett. These are not biases you can simply block because, after all, we're only human. But as investors, one thing we can control is whether we let these biases influence our decision-making. Once you acknowledge that you will be affected by these behavioral biases, you unlock an investing superpower: the ability to understand your emotions and thus, the ability to detach from them when making decisions. So, keep these six "killers of wealth" front of mind. The goal is not to eliminate them (because that is impossible), but to recognize when they are influencing your thinking. And when you notice that happening, remember to slow down, take a step back, and separate the emotional brain from the rational one.

In the end, investing success is not about perfection or intelligence. It comes from self-awareness and consistent rationality, the same qualities that allow Warren Buffett to quietly sit in his Omaha office, reading annual reports and making decisions free from the emotional noise of Wall Street.

EVEN THE PROS FALL VICTIM

It's tempting to believe that emotional investing is a retail investor problem. That it's the average person, not the professionals, who falls prey to fear, greed, and short-term thinking. But the reality is, even the most experienced fund managers are vulnerable. In fact, in many ways, they're *more* vulnerable because they're not just investing with their own money like us. They're playing a different game altogether.

This might sound ridiculous, but it's true: professional money managers aren't solely in the business of generating long-term returns for their clients. While that still is a core part of their job, professional money managers are predominantly in the business of *retaining clients*. And that changes everything.

You see, most fund managers are not judged over 5 or 10 years but are examined quarter by quarter. Their careers depend on how their performance stacks up against their peers right now. If they underperform the benchmark for even a few months, clients start pulling money. I mean, why would their clients stay invested with them if their competitor across the street is generating better returns? Because of this inescapable trap, the fund manager's eyes commonly shift away from analyzing businesses and instead shift toward their competitor's homework. What the fund managers really want to examine are the holdings of all the other fund managers, and as Charlie Munger would say, "Mimicking the herd invites regression to the mean."

This explains why fund managers often hug the benchmark index, why they rotate into trendy sectors, and why they pile into whatever's hot. They're not thinking like business owners; they're thinking like career managers trying to avoid embarrassment. The system punishes independent thinking and rewards conformity, even when it's completely irrational.

This pressure naturally leads to emotional decision-making, even among the smartest people in the room.

And the numbers bear this out: over a 10-year period, *about 86% of actively managed funds underperform the market* (S&P Dow Jones Indices, 2025). Yes, you read that correctly. These are highly educated professionals, often with teams of analysts and access to vast data, and yet they still trail the market return. (See Figure 3.1.)

Why? Because they're human.

Figure 3.1   Percentage of all large-cap funds that underperformed the S&P 500.

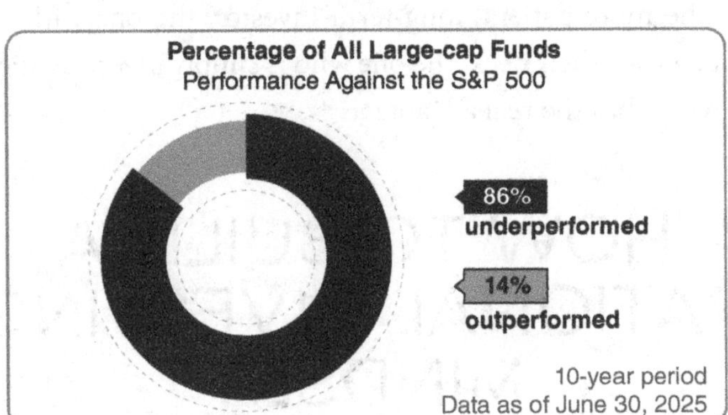

Just like retail investors, they're susceptible to the same cognitive traps: overconfidence, herding, recency bias, and loss aversion. You can see this play out in countless real-world examples.

During the dot-com mania of the late 1990s, even seasoned fund managers abandoned valuation discipline to chase internet stocks that had no earnings and no business model. They didn't want to be the only ones missing out. When the bubble burst, they went down with everyone else.

More recently, the ARK Innovation Fund became a poster child for emotional investing. In 2020 and 2021, it attracted billions of dollars as it loaded up on high-growth, speculative tech names. The manager, Cathie Wood, was hailed as a visionary. But when the macro environment shifted and interest rates rose, the fund collapsed, dropping more than 70% from its highs. The strategy didn't change. The story just stopped working.

These examples aren't about intelligence; they're about temperament. They serve as a reminder that even the pros, with all their resources and credentials, can fall into the same psychological traps as any other investor.

So don't assume that following the professionals is always a safe bet. In many cases, they're reacting to pressure, not thinking clearly. In fact, the more patient, long-term investor, the one with nobody breathing down their neck, the one who is simply investing their own money, often has the real advantage.

HOW TO BUILD A RATIONAL INVESTING MINDSET

So, what should you take from all of this? The main lesson is that succeeding in the market requires more than just financial knowledge. You also need the discipline to stay calm when others panic and patient when others rush. The good news is that temperament is not something you either have or don't. Like any skill, it can be developed over time with the right tools and habits.

So, to close this chapter, I want to share five key lessons I have learned from studying the world's greatest investors that have helped me master my emotions and make better decisions. These are lessons I have written down, pinned to my wall, and leaned on through every market swing of the past decade. They may not tell you which stocks to buy or sell, but they will help you build the one thing that matters most: a steady temperament that keeps you grounded and well positioned to create wealth over the long term.

1. Understand That You Are Biased

The first step to becoming a rational investor is recognizing a simple, uncomfortable truth: you are biased. So is every other investor.

These biases aren't flaws in your character; they're part of being human. Our brains evolved to make quick decisions, to seek patterns, to fear loss more than we value gain. That might help you avoid danger in the wild, but as we discussed, in the stock market, it can lead to overconfidence, panic selling, chasing past winners, or ignoring inconvenient facts.

The goal here isn't to eliminate your biases. What you need to be able to do is *notice* them. To pause when you feel the urge to act emotionally. To ask, "Am I reacting to data, or just to fear? Am I being objective, or just looking for information that confirms what I already want to believe?" Warren Buffett and Charlie Munger mentioned throughout their careers the importance of developing a mental framework that allowed them to step outside their instincts and think rationally. You can't stop the bias from appearing, but you can choose not to act on it.

2. Not Every Investment Will Be a Winner

Even Warren Buffett (the greatest investor of all time) has made plenty of bad investments: Dexter Shoe, IBM, the airline industry (twice). Mistakes are part of the game. What sets great investors apart isn't perfection; rather, it's how they respond when they realize they're wrong.

The key is to reevaluate. If the facts have changed, and if the business is no longer what you thought it was, don't cling to your original thesis out of pride. Take action. Exit and move on. (We'll talk more about when to sell later.) But just as important is accepting, *from the outset*, that you won't get every call right.

Buffett himself has said that most of Berkshire Hathaway's success boils down to just a dozen truly great decisions. That's roughly one every five years. A dozen great calls, surrounded by countless mediocre ones, yet he's averaged around 20% per year since 1965. That's the power of letting your winners run and not letting your losers destroy you. You don't need to be right every time. You just need to make sure your biggest winners have room to shine, and that you're humble enough to admit when you're wrong.

3.   You Can Never Predict a Downturn

One of the biggest mistakes investors make is thinking they can outsmart the market. They try to sell before a crash, buy back in at the bottom, and dodge every headline risk in between. But the truth is, no one can consistently predict when a downturn will happen. Not economists, not analysts, not even the best investors in the world.

Market drops are part of the investing experience. They will happen, but they won't arrive with a calendar invite. Trying to anticipate them usually leads to missed opportunities, emotional decision-making, and poor long-term results.

The better approach is to stop guessing and start preparing. If you accept that downturns are inevitable, you can build your portfolio and mindset in a way that can handle them. Rational investors don't try to avoid every bump in the road. They focus on making sound decisions, staying calm through volatility, and letting time do the heavy lifting.

4.   Prepare to Endure Multiple 30% Market Drops

If you invest for long enough, you will experience your portfolio falling by 30% or more. Honestly, probably more than a few times if you're invested for a decent length of time. (I've already seen a few.) That's not unusual. In fact, it's completely normal. Sharp declines are part of how markets work.

These moments can be emotionally tough. Headlines will scream panic, and people around you may start selling. But history shows that these drops happen regularly. They're not signs that something is broken. They're the cost of participating in a system that, over time, builds wealth.

After the Great Recession of 2007–2009, Charlie Munger was interviewed by the BBC and asked, "How worried are you by the declines in the share price of Berkshire Hathaway?" His response was blunt:

"Zero. This is the third time that Warren and I have seen our holdings in Berkshire go down top-tick to bottom-tick by 50%. I think it's in the nature of long-term shareholding, with the natural vicissitudes and worldly outcomes in markets, that the long-term holder has the quoted value of his stock go down by, say, 50%. You can argue that if you're not willing to react with equanimity to a market price decline of 50%, two or three times a century, you're not fit to be a common shareholder, and you deserve the mediocre result you're going to get."

What separates successful investors is not that they avoid down-turns but that they learn to sit through them. Warren Buffett has seen countless market tumbles over his career, but he never panicked. He understood that if the underlying businesses were still strong, the price would eventually recover.

To invest well, you need to expect volatility, not fear it. And when those big drops happen, remind yourself that they're part of the journey. You can't get long-term results without short-term discomfort.

5.   In the Short Term, the Market Is a Voting Machine; in the Long Run, It Is a Weighing Machine

In the short term, stock prices are driven by popularity. News cycles, investor sentiment, hype, fear, and momentum all play a role in moving prices up and down each day (just think GameStop). The market acts like a voting machine, recording what is popular rather than what is valuable.

But as investors, it's important to understand that in the long run, this is *not* what drives prices. Over time, the long-term trend of a stock will *always* be based on underlying business performance. The true strength of a business (its earnings, growth, and competitive position) will shine through. Over time, the market becomes a weighing machine, slowly measuring substance instead of noise.

This idea, first introduced by Benjamin Graham and often repeated by Warren Buffett, is a reminder to focus on business fundamentals. It can be easy to get caught up in short-term price movements, but in the long run, it is the underlying performance of the business that ultimately determines its value.

Rational investors understand this. They tune out the day-to-day distractions and concentrate on the quality of the companies they own. Because while popularity can change prices in a moment, true value is what shines through in the long run.

THE BIG PICTURE

At the end of the day, great investing is not about outsmarting everyone else. It is about outlasting them. And the ability to stay invested through all market conditions for long periods of time ultimately depends on one thing: your temperament.

As noted earlier, Warren Buffett has said that most of Berkshire Hathaway's success can be traced back to just a dozen or so great decisions over several decades. Not hundreds. Not thousands. Just a small handful of high-conviction choices, made with patience, and held through thick and thin.

Success in investing doesn't come from reacting faster, it comes from reacting *less*. It comes from tuning out the noise, trusting your process, and giving compounding the time it needs to do its work. That's the mindset every investor must embrace before truly beginning their journey.

In this way, the stock market is quite paradoxical. It's ultimately the world's obsession with speed, dopamine, and getting rich quick that creates the very opportunities long-term investors take advantage of. As Warren Buffett put it at Berkshire's 2023 shareholder meeting:

> What gives you opportunities is other people doing dumb things … and over the years, there's been a great increase in people doing big, dumb things.

These emotionally driven moments—fear, panic, greed—are the cracks in the market where value slips through. For the rational investor, that's when the market starts raining gold. And it's the ability to act calmly in those moments that ultimately separates the great investors from the rest of the pack.

STEP 2

LAY THE FOUNDATION

CHAPTER FOUR

THE MOST COMMON INVESTING STRATEGY IN THE WORLD

With the preparation stage behind us, now comes the exciting part. The next step is to start investing. Step 2 of *The New Money Strategy* focuses on laying the foundation for your long-term wealth.

Just like a house needs a solid concrete slab to stand the test of time, your financial plan needs a strong base to support long-term growth. And while it's true that you may get lucky building on shaky ground, luck is simply not a robust strategy in the stock market. So how do we lay the concrete supports of our financial future? Buffett-style investors typically build their foundation through a strategy called "passive investing."

PASSIVE INVESTING

What is passive investing? Simply put, it's the strategy of buying a little bit of everything and going along for the ride, as opposed to buying individual stocks and trying to pick the market's winners.

Passive investors do not try to beat the market. Instead, they aim to match the market's returns by buying into index funds that mirror the performance of an index such as the S&P 500. They are content to ride the ups and downs of the market, confident that over time, corporate America will continue to grow and create value.

Active investors, on the other hand, make investment decisions in an attempt to outperform the market. Rather than simply going along for the ride, they want to take the wheel. They buy and sell individual stocks, bonds, cryptocurrencies, or other assets, all with the goal of achieving returns higher than a benchmark index (like the S&P 500).

Interestingly, while Warren Buffett himself has spent his career actively picking stocks through Berkshire Hathaway, he has long recommended a very different approach for everyday investors. In fact, he regularly points to passive investing as the smartest long-term investment strategy for most people.

In his 2016 shareholder letter, he wrote:

Over the years, I've often been asked for investment advice, and in the process of answering I've learned a good deal about human behavior. My regular recommendation has been a low-cost S&P 500 index fund. To their credit, my friends who possess only modest means have usually followed my suggestion.

This is the essence of passive investing. It's simple, effective, and incredibly powerful for building long-term wealth. Buffett reinforced this message again in his 2013 letter, writing:

> You don't need to be an expert in order to achieve satisfactory investment returns. But if you aren't, you must recognize your limitations and follow a course certain to work reasonably well.

But how do we implement this "passive investing" strategy Buffett advises? What is a "low-cost S&P 500 index fund," and how do we structure this part of our portfolio to minimize our risk of losses? Well, before we answer these questions, we first need to understand the stock market itself.

In the United States, there are around 4,000–4,500 publicly traded companies (companies the general public can buy shares in). These range from household names like Johnson & Johnson and Procter & Gamble to tech giants like Tesla, Apple, and Nvidia. Because there are so many companies to follow, investors commonly sort these companies into groups known as indexes (or indices—both terms are used frequently on Wall Street) to track different parts of the market.

These indexes are not naturally occurring. We make them up, based on what we're trying to track. For example, you can group companies by their size, by their industry, by their dividend payouts—really you can group these companies based on anything:

- **The Russell 2000** tracks 2,000 small-cap US companies. The up and down movement of this index offers insight into the performance of smaller businesses without the influence of larger corporations.
- **The Dow Jones Industrial Average** tracks 30 large, established companies from a variety of industries, such as McDonald's, Coca-Cola, and Boeing.
- **The S&P 500** (by far the most commonly referenced index) represents the 500 largest companies in America. This includes

nearly every major name in corporate America: Apple, Google (Alphabet), Nvidia, Tesla, Microsoft, Meta, Amazon, Berkshire Hathaway, Walmart, JP Morgan, and many more.

While investors have made up a mind-boggling amount of "indexes," there is one that commonly stands above the rest. Whenever the media or Wall Street talks about "the market" being up or down, they are almost always referring to the S&P 500 index, the group of the 500 largest companies in America.

But how does this relate to passive investing?

Passive investors will typically spread their money across the businesses within the S&P 500 index, as this index has a long history of strong performance. Since 1957, the S&P 500 index has returned an average of 10.33% annually (not adjusted for inflation), and while we can never be sure of what the future holds, passive investors hope that the future of the S&P 500 will look somewhat like its past (Investopedia, 2025). They hope that the rising tide of corporate America will continue to lift all boats, and thus, owning even a small amount of America's 500 biggest and best companies will continue to be a solid wealth-building strategy.

"I don't know Brandon. That seems dangerous. Won't there be a lot of losers out of those 500 companies? Wouldn't it be better to trust my money with a fund manager, who is more likely to see the winners and losers coming?"

On the surface, that seems like a very logical question, and I want to take a moment to address why this doesn't work out. Firstly, yes. There will be many companies in the S&P 500 that will fail. Enron was part of the S&P 500 back in the late 1990s before it famously went bust. But it's the wide diversification of the index that absorbs the blow. With 500 of America's biggest and best making up the index, one company falling from grace is simply not enough to significantly impact the index, and remember, once a poor performing company's market cap falls far enough, they will simply be tossed out, replaced by the company that was, previously, the 501st largest company in America.

In this way, the index has a "self-cleaning" function, tossing out the very poor performers and welcoming the up and comers. This helps to protect the index. Remember, the "10.33% annual return since 1957" is inclusive of *all* market events. It includes all the financial crises (such as the 2008 global financial crisis), it includes massive companies (like Enron) falling from grace, and it includes every down day, every earnings downgrade, every scandal, every negative event you could possibly think of.

But passive investors don't dwell on the negatives. They're not trying to pick the winners and avoid the losers. They simply trust that the overarching strength of corporate America will continue to lift their diversified portfolio over time.

So, should you hand over your hard-earned money to a fund manager instead?

Well, I don't want to throw too much criticism at money managers (after all I know a lot of exceptional money managers who do beat the market), but the reality is: probably not. As we discussed in the prior chapter, according to S&P Global's SPIVA Scorecard, over the past 10 years, a whopping 86% of actively managed funds have underperformed the S&P 500 (S&P Dow Jones Indices, 2025). For this reason, when it comes to building the foundation of my passive investing portfolio, I am much more inclined to do it myself rather than being charged 2% annually for someone else to do it for me (and probably get a worse outcome).

In fact, this sobering data from SPIVA has led to growing pressure on asset managers globally to shift away from active stock-picking and toward the simple, reliable strategy that Warren Buffett recommends: passive investing. And the numbers show just how quickly this shift has accelerated. Between 2015 and 2024, passively managed funds attracted $5.8 trillion in net new money, while active funds saw a net outflow of $2.5 trillion (Kerzérho, 2025). Today, 53% of all fund assets are managed passively, compared to 47% actively, a reversal that would have seemed unthinkable just 30 years ago (Kerzérho, 2025).

UNDERSTANDING EXCHANGE-TRADED FUNDS

Okay, so we've established that Warren Buffett's recommendation for everyday investors is to stop trying to beat the market and instead just go along for the ride. We're on board. Passive investing sounds like a plan. Participating in the market, riding its ups and downs, and trusting that the future of corporate America will somewhat resemble the past. Historically, that approach has delivered an average annual return of around 10%.

But how do you implement this strategy? While the S&P 500 is the most commonly used index to track "the market," you can't buy shares in the index itself. An index is not a company. It's simply a list of businesses grouped together for tracking and comparison purposes. And buying into 500 companies individually is a logistical nightmare, not to mention the brokerage cost of 500 individual trades.

So how do investors "buy the index"? The answer is through ETFs, or exchange-traded funds.

An ETF is an investment product designed to mimic the performance of an underlying index, such as the S&P 500. It does this by investing in the same companies the index tracks. Put simply, when you buy one share of an ETF that mimics the S&P 500, you're not just buying one company, you're buying a small slice of all 500 companies in that index, bundled into one, easy investment.

ETFs trade on stock exchanges just like regular company shares. This means you can buy and sell them throughout the trading day at current market prices. It also means you can start investing with a relatively small amount and gradually build your position over time. This flexibility, combined with the instant diversification ETFs provide, is a big part of their popularity.

Take VOO as an example. This is a Vanguard ETF that tracks the S&P 500. With one purchase, you gain exposure to Apple, Microsoft, Amazon, Alphabet, Tesla, and hundreds of other major US companies. Instead of trying to pick which of these will outperform, you're choosing to own the entire group and let long-term performance work in your favor. (See Table 4.1.)

This is the real advantage of passive investing. It gives you broad access to high-quality companies while keeping your costs incredibly low. VOO, for example, charges an annual fee of just 0.03% (at the time of writing) (Vanguard, 2025). This means a $10,000 investment would cost you only $3 per year in fees, compared to hundreds of dollars in fees charged by actively managed funds offering similar exposure.

It's worth understanding, however, that not all ETFs are created equal. In the early days, ETFs were simple investment tools designed

Table 4.1 VOO Mimicking the S&P 500 Index

	1 Year Return (%)	3 Year Return (%)	5 Year Return (%)	10 Year Return (%)	Return Since Inception (%)
VOO (Market Price)	15.96	19.53	14.70	14.57	14.70
S&P 500 Index	15.88	19.54	14.74	14.60	14.74

Source: Vanguard, 2025

to mirror the performance of major indexes, like the S&P 500. But as passive investing grew in popularity, ETF providers naturally began offering more products under the "ETF" label. But the truth is, many of these newer options have very little to do with passive investing at all.

At its core, an ETF is just a basket of stocks selected based on a specific investment objective. For example, VOO is a basket of the 500 largest companies in the United States because its objective is to replicate the performance of the S&P 500 index.

These days, however, investment objectives are getting more complicated. In fact, some ETFs, particularly the so-called "thematic ETFs," resemble active investing much more than passive investing.

Take BlackRock's iShares US Healthcare ETF (IYH) as an example. The stated investment objective on their website is:

> The iShares US Healthcare ETF seeks to track the investment results of an index composed of U.S. equities in the healthcare sector. (BlackRock, 2025)

So far, that sounds reasonable. But dig a little deeper, and you'll find that the index being tracked is called the Russell 1000 Health Care RIC 22.5/45 Capped Index, which frankly sounds more like a piece of hospital equipment than a stock market benchmark.

What does that name actually mean? Good question. It turns out this is a custom-built index made up of healthcare companies within the Russell 1000. The "RIC 22.5/45 Capped" part refers to a rule under the Investment Company Act of 1940, which governs tax-advantaged funds. Under these rules, no single company can make up more than 22.5% of the total index, and all companies that individually account for more than 5% cannot collectively exceed 45%.

Confused yet? I am. Take me back to the S&P 500, thanks. This is a perfect example of how far some modern ETF products have drifted from the roots of passive investing.

Now, to be clear, I'm not saying IYH is a bad investment. I'm not telling anyone to avoid the iShares US Healthcare ETF. What I am saying is that when you buy something like this, you need to understand what you're doing. You're not just participating in the broader market anymore. You're making a bet. By buying IYH, you're saying you believe that a select group of large US healthcare companies will perform better than the market overall. And that's certainly not the approach that Buffett was talking about.

Believe it or not, in today's ETF landscape, IYH is actually one of the milder examples. These days, you can find ETFs so narrowly focused that a healthcare bet starts to look boring by comparison.

Here are just a few:

- **iShares U.S. Aerospace & Defense ETF (ITA)**
  Provides exposure to US companies in the aerospace, weapons, and defense sector, including major players like Lockheed Martin and Raytheon.
- **Bitwise Crypto Industry Innovators ETF (BITQ)**
  Tracks the Bitwise Crypto Innovators 30 Index, offering exposure to companies hoping to build the crypto economy, such as Coinbase and Strategy (formerly MicroStrategy).
- **VanEck Social Sentiment ETF (BUZZ)**
  Selects stocks based on positive social media sentiment, including meme stocks like GameStop and AMC, and other buzzworthy names like Reddit, Robinhood, and Rivian.

These are clearly not broad-based investments. They are focused bets on narrow themes, specific industries, or even internet hype. Yet time and time again, investors hoping to invest passively are led astray by these kinds of ETF products, and it costs them. Not just in the form of long-term underperformance, but also in higher fees.

Take VOO, the simple S&P 500 index fund we discussed earlier. It has an annual expense ratio of just 0.03%. In comparison, ITA, BITQ, and BUZZ charge 0.40%, 0.85%, and 0.76%, respectively. That's more than 10 times the cost of a broad-market fund, a steep premium to pay for what is, at its core, a speculative bet.

CHOOSING THE RIGHT ETF

So that leads us to an important question: How do you choose the right ETF for you? How do you decide which investments will form the backbone of your portfolio?

Every investor is different. We have different goals, live in different countries, and have access to different investment platforms and markets. There's no one-size-fits-all answer, but there are some timeless principles that can guide you toward the right choice.

With that in mind, here are five key considerations to help you choose the ETF that best suits your needs and sets you up for long-term success.

1.   Go Broad, Not Niche

If you're building the foundation of a passive investment strategy, the first rule is simple: stick with broad-market ETFs.

Broad-market ETFs are designed to track large, diversified segments of the market. They give you exposure to hundreds, or even thousands, of companies in a single investment. These are the types of ETFs that Warren Buffett recommends for the everyday investor: simple, low-cost, and effective.

These types of funds are well-diversified, time-tested, and come with very low fees. Most importantly, they align with Warren Buffett's advice to everyday investors: don't try to beat the market, just participate in it as broadly and efficiently as possible.

Table 4.2 Common S&P 500 ETFs

Ticker	Fund Name	Provider	Expense Ratio (%)	Assets Under Management (AUM)
SPY	SPDR S&P 500 ETF Trust	State Street Global Advisors	0.0945	$640.4 billion
IVV	iShares Core S&P 500 ETF	BlackRock (iShares)	0.03	$633.0 billion
VOO	Vanguard S&P 500 ETF	Vanguard	0.03	$656.8 billion

Source: State Street Global Advisors, 2025; BlackRock/iShares, 2025; Vanguard, 2025

For many investors, especially those with easy access to US-listed ETFs, owning a simple S&P 500 index fund might be all you ever need. That's exactly what Warren Buffett recommends for most people. And if it's good enough for the GOAT, it's probably good enough for the rest of us too.

With that in mind, Table 4.2 shows three of the most popular S&P 500 index funds for your consideration.

But here is an important nuance. While a widely diversified US market ETF might be all you need, it is also perfectly reasonable to tailor your approach based on what you know best.

For example, I live in Australia. I have grown up hearing about local companies, observing how the Australian economy works, and understanding the culture around business and investing down under. So, for me, my version of "broad" includes a combination of VAS (which tracks the Australian share market) and an Australian domiciled version of IVV (which tracks the S&P 500). Together, these give me strong domestic exposure along with access to the world's largest economy, and it's a portfolio I understand and feel comfortable with.

This kind of tailoring does not go against the principles of passive investing. In fact, it can strengthen them. When you invest in what you understand, you are more likely to stay the course. The key is to stick with broad, market-tracking ETFs rather than chasing niche themes or making bets that require constant monitoring or special insight.

To sum it up: go broad, and if you can, go familiar too. That is how you build conviction, stay invested for the long run, and give your wealth the best chance to grow steadily over time. That is what passive investing is all about.

2.   Check the Fee

One of the biggest advantages of passive investing is that it's cheap, or at least, it should be.

As we've discussed, every ETF charges a small annual fee called an "expense ratio." This fee covers the cost of managing the fund and is taken automatically from the fund's assets. You don't pay it directly, but it quietly reduces your returns over time.

For example, an ETF with a 0.03% expense ratio (like VOO) will cost you just $3 per year on a $10,000 investment. Compare that to a thematic ETF charging 0.80%. That same $10,000 would cost you $80 per year. It may not sound like much, but over decades, the difference becomes significant.

As a rule of thumb, for your core long-term holdings, look for an ETF with an expense ratio under 0.10%. The lower, the better. These ultra-low-cost funds tend to track large, established indexes and are built for investors who want to keep more of their returns.

Fees are one of the few things you can control as an investor, so always check it. If it's high, forget it. There are plenty of options out there for what we're trying to achieve.

3.   Understand the Index It Tracks

Not all ETFs are created equal, even if they sound similar on the surface. One of the most important things you can do before investing in an ETF is to understand what index it really tracks.

This information should be clearly stated in the ETFs investment objective, which should be easily found on the fund's webpage or factsheet. It will say something like, "This fund seeks to track the performance of the S&P 500" or "This fund aims to replicate the Russell 1000 Value Index." Don't skip this part. The index is the blueprint for what you're investing in.

Take the S&P 500 and the Russell 1000 Value Index as an example. (See Table 4.3.) They both invest in large US companies, but they are built very differently. The S&P 500 includes the 500 largest US companies regardless of style, sector, or growth rate. It gives you broad exposure to the entire US economy.

The Russell 1000 Value Index, on the other hand, only includes companies from the Russell 1000 (the 1,000 largest US companies) that meet certain "value" criteria (meaning they trade at lower prices relative to their fundamentals). That index intentionally avoids faster growing or more expensive companies like Nvidia or Tesla.

Table 4.3 Top 10 Holdings of the S&P 500 vs Russell 1000 Value Index

Position	S&P 500	Russell 1000 Value Index
1	Nvidia	Berkshire Hathaway (Class B)
2	Microsoft	JP Morgan Chase
3	Apple	Amazon
4	Amazon	Alphabet Inc (Class A)
5	Meta Platforms	Exxon Mobil
6	Broadcom	Johnson & Johnson
7	Alphabet Inc (Class A)	Alphabet Inc (Class C)
8	Tesla	Walmart
9	Alphabet Inc (Class C)	Procter & Gamble
10	Berkshire Hathaway	Bank of America

In other words, a fund that tracks the Russell 1000 Value Index will look very different from one that tracks the S&P 500. It may perform better in some years, worse in others, and it will carry different sector weights and risk exposures.

So always check the index. Read a short summary of what it includes and how it is built. If it's broad, market-weighted, and diversified, it's likely a solid foundation. If it's narrowly focused or based on specific filters, understand that it doesn't fit the passive investing criteria Buffett recommends.

4.   Look at the Top Holdings

Every ETF is made up of a group of individual investments. So even if the name and description sound good, it's worth digging one step deeper to see what you're actually buying.

A simple habit that can go a long way is checking the ETF's top 10 holdings. This list is usually available on the provider's website or any major financial data platform. It shows the largest positions the fund holds and often gives you a snapshot of how the ETF is constructed.

In fact, for a broad-market ETF like IVV (which tracks the S&P 500), the top 10 holdings should look identical to the top 10 holdings of the S&P 500 index. Table 4.4 shows the top 10 stocks in the S&P 500, and Table 4.5 shows the top 10 holdings of IVV (as of 1 October 2025).

As you can see, the top 10 holdings of the S&P 500 index and IVV are identical, but there are slight differences in the weightings. This is perfectly normal. Even though ETFs like IVV are designed to closely mirror the S&P 500, there will always be small discrepancies. The most common reason is timing. Index data and ETF holdings are often updated on different days, and in volatile markets, a few days can shift company rankings based on price changes. The S&P 500 is also rebalanced periodically, and while changes are announced ahead

Table 4.4   S&P 500 Top 10 Stocks

	Company	Symbol	Weight (%)
1	Nvidia	NVDA	7.51
2	Microsoft	MSFT	6.36
3	Apple	AAPL	6.25
4	Amazon	AMZN	3.87
5	Meta Platforms	META	3.05
6	Broadcom	AVGO	2.58
7	Alphabet Inc. (Class A)	GOOGL	2.51
8	Tesla	TSLA	2.44
9	Alphabet Inc. (Class C)	GOOG	2.35
10	Berkshire Hathaway (Class B)	BRK.B	1.79

Adapted from (SlickCharts, 2025)

Table 4.5   Top 10 Holdings of IVV

	Company	Symbol	Weight (%)
1	Nvidia	NVDA	7.80
2	Microsoft	MSFT	6.72
3	Apple	AAPL	6.64
4	Amazon	AMZN	3.79
5	Meta Platforms	META	2.83
6	Broadcom	AVGO	2.71
7	Alphabet Inc. (Class A)	GOOGL	2.49
8	Tesla	TSLA	2.19
9	Alphabet Inc. (Class C)	GOOG	2.01
10	Berkshire Hathaway	BRK.B	1.61

Adapted from (BlackRock/iShares, 2025)

of time, ETFs may take a few days to fully adjust. These small differences are, however, no cause for concern. Over time, funds like IVV have tracked their target indexes with remarkable accuracy, and any temporary mismatches tend to be minimal and short-lived.

Overall, getting into the habit of checking the top holdings is a smart way to stay informed. For broad-market ETFs, it helps confirm that you're actually getting diversified exposure to the biggest names in the market. And for more specialized ETFs, it can reveal just how concentrated or thematic the fund really is. You might be surprised to find that what sounds like a balanced investment on the surface is actually weighted heavily toward just a handful of companies. In short, always look under the hood. It takes just a minute but gives you a clearer picture of what you actually own. And when it comes to investing for the long term, that kind of clarity matters.

5.   Avoid Overlap and Complexity

Once you discover how many ETFs are out there, it can be tempting to build a large, varied collection. Trust me, I've been there. But more doesn't always mean better. In fact, owning too many ETFs often leads to unnecessary overlap, where you just end up holding the same companies through multiple funds.

For example, if you own both an S&P 500 ETF and a Nasdaq-100 ETF, you'll find significant duplication in the top holdings. Companies like Apple, Microsoft, Nvidia, and Amazon appear prominently in both. In this case, you're not truly diversifying. You're just adding layers of complexity, and that's something we want to avoid.

Warren Buffett has long been an advocate for simplicity. One of his best-known quotes is, "There seems to be some perverse human characteristic that likes to make easy things difficult." Complexity might feel sophisticated, but in investing, it usually adds confusion and risk. A cluttered portfolio makes it harder to understand what you own, how it's performing, and why you own it in the first place.

The fee-collecting Wall Street types will hate me for saying this, but the truth is that you only need one ETF to build a strong, long-term portfolio. A single low-cost, broad-market index fund (like one that tracks the S&P 500) gives you instant exposure to hundreds of the world's most valuable companies, across a range of industries.

Too often, beginners are made to feel like they're not doing enough. But in passive investing, less is often more. A simple, focused approach—especially one built around a single broad-market ETF—can be more effective, more resilient, and far easier to stick with over the long run.

That's exactly what we are aiming for when building the foundation of our portfolio. The goal is to find one, two, or at most three reliable, long-term ETFs that are broad, diversified, and set up to quietly grow our wealth over time. If we get this part right, the passive investing core will always be working in the background.

And that is what makes it so powerful. No matter what happens in the economy, the markets, or your personal life, you will have something strong and steady helping you build wealth. It becomes your financial safety net. A base to build on, a cushion when things go wrong, and a quiet force that keeps pushing you forward when things go right.

Passive investing may not be exciting, but it is simple, proven, and consistent. For most people, that is exactly what works.

CHAPTER FIVE

SETTING UP YOUR STRATEGY

When it comes to building a solid foundation through passive investing, choosing the right exchange-traded fund (ETF) is like selecting the concrete and steel. But once you've gathered the materials, you still need to build. So how do passive investors actually put this strategy into action and stay on track to capture the average market return over time? The key is a method called dollar-cost averaging. It's a simple but powerful process that transforms good intentions into consistent results.

UNDERSTANDING DOLLAR-COST AVERAGING

Despite the confusing name, dollar-cost averaging is a very simple idea. All it means is investing a fixed amount of money at regular intervals, regardless of what the market is doing. No guessing. No waiting for the perfect moment. Just showing up, over and over again. That might mean investing $100 every week, $2,000 every quarter, or $5,000 once a year. The amount and timing are both up to you. What matters most is consistency. See Figure 5.1.

Why do we do it this way? Because dollar-cost averaging helps you let go of the illusion that you can time the market. You stop worrying about whether prices are high or low, and you focus instead on the habit of investing.

Figure 5.1   Dollar-cost averaging $500 per month.

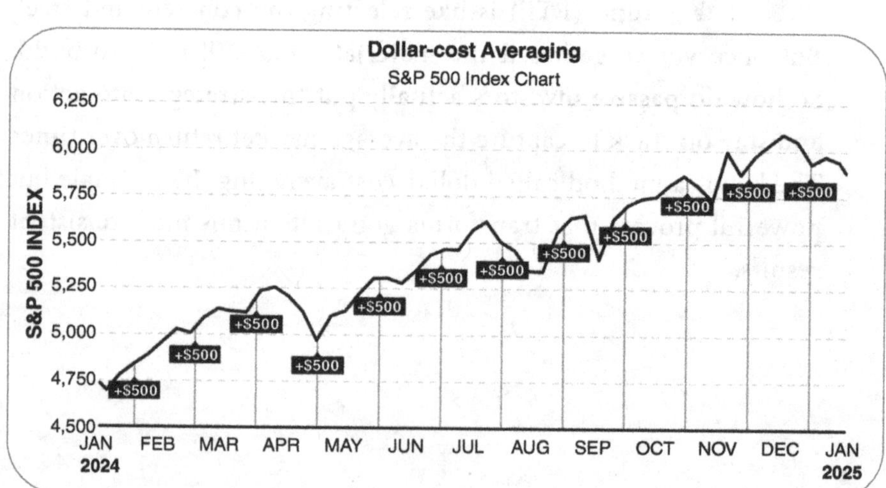

Over time, this approach provides three major benefits. First, it removes emotion from your decision-making. Second, it naturally leads you to buy more shares when prices are low and fewer when they are high. And third, it allows you to gradually capture the *average* return of the market over the long term, which is exactly what passive investing is all about.

Interestingly, dollar-cost averaging is also the strategy Warren Buffett recommends for passive investors. Back at the 2002 Berkshire Hathaway Shareholder Meeting, Buffett said:

> I would pick a broad index, but I wouldn't toss a chunk in at any one time. I would do it over a period of time because the very nature of index funds is that you are saying: I think America's business is going to do well over a long period of time, but I don't know enough to pick the winners and I don't know enough to pick the winning times.

It might sound like an overly simple strategy, but don't underestimate the power of consistency. For example, imagine you decide to invest $100 every single week into a low-cost, broad-market ETF. You don't try to time the market. You don't adjust based on headlines. You just stick with your plan and keep investing that same amount, week in, week out.

Say you keep this up for 40 years. Over that time, you would have invested a total of $208,000. Now that's a serious commitment, but not an unrealistic one. For many people, $100 a week is manageable, especially as income grows over time.

But here's the magic: if your investment earns the long-term historical average of the S&P 500, which is around 10% per year, your $208,000 doesn't just grow. It multiplies. Thanks to the power of compounding, that consistent weekly investment could grow to more than $2.41 million over 40 years. You read that right: $208,000 in, over $2.4 million out. That's the kind of deal long-term investors

Figure 5.2   Forty years of passive investing $100 per week.

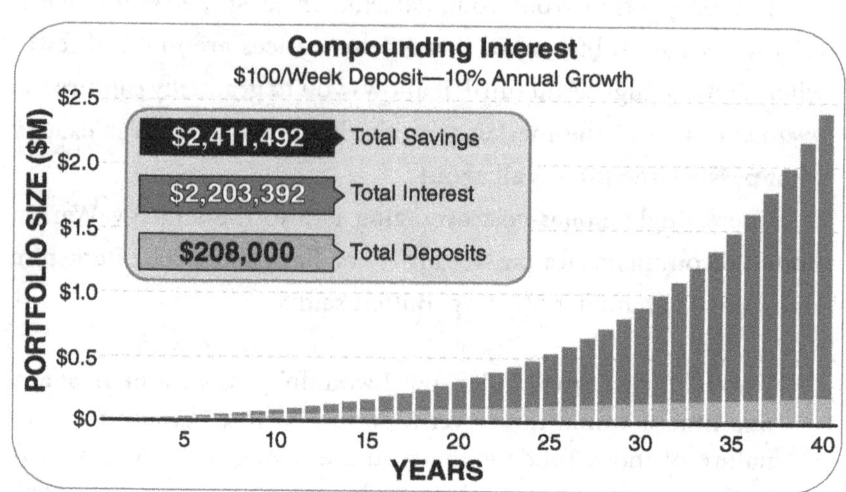

dream of. Figure 5.2 shows it clearly. The gradation at the bottom shows your total invested cash, while the upper gradation that keeps arcing higher shows the compound interest earned over time.

This is achieved without ever needing to pick stocks, make predictions, or do anything complicated. You didn't have to be right about when to buy or sell. You just had to show up and invest consistently.

This is the quiet power of dollar-cost averaging. It is not flashy. It is not something you will hear about on the evening news. But historically, it has worked exceptionally well. It works because it is steady, boring, and built on discipline.

This is by far the biggest advantage of the approach. When you commit to investing a fixed amount on a regular schedule, you stop worrying about whether now is the "right time." You're not trying to predict the market or second-guess your decisions. You're simply implementing a system that runs quietly in the background, no matter what the headlines say.

There's a popular story that Fidelity once studied its top-performing investment accounts and found that the best results came from people who either forgot they had an account or had passed away. While there's no hard evidence this study ever existed, the idea still rings true. When it comes to investing, we are often our own worst enemy. But passive investors sidestep that trap. By removing the urge to tinker, dollar-cost averaging helps you stay the course, and that discipline is what builds real wealth over time.

Beyond reducing stress, dollar-cost averaging also has a powerful mathematical effect too. Because you're investing the same dollar amount regularly, you will naturally buy more shares when prices are low and fewer shares when prices are high. Over time, this can result in a lower average cost per share than if you had invested one large lump sum at a random time.

Here's a simple way to think about it. Let's say you invest $1,000 each month, and the price of your chosen ETF fluctuates like this (also shown in Figure 5.3):

- Month 1: $100 per share → you buy 10 shares
- Month 2: $50 per share → you buy 20 shares
- Month 3: $200 per share → you buy 5 shares

Figure 5.3 Dollar-cost averaging during share price fluctuations.

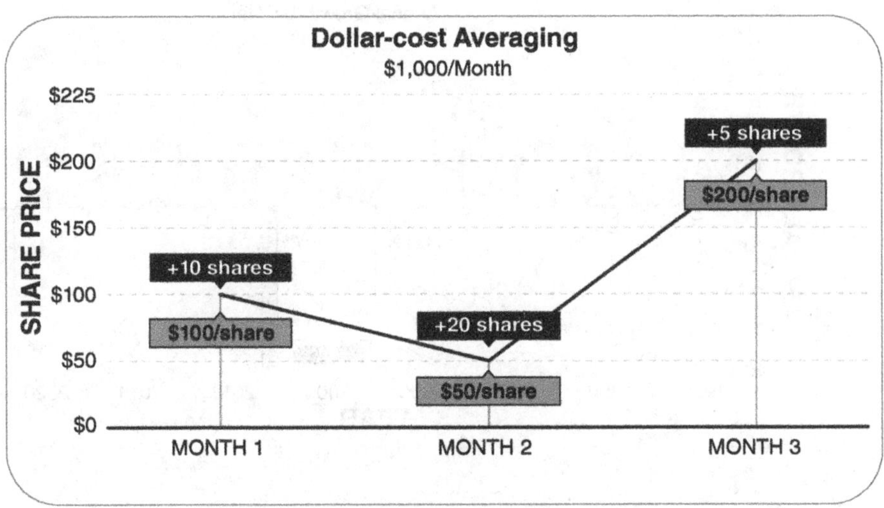

Over three months, you've invested $3,000 and accumulated 35 shares in total. That puts your average cost per share at roughly $85.70 even though the stock price was $100 or more for two of those months. That's the quiet magic of dollar-cost averaging. You end up buying more when prices are low and less when they're high, without needing to time the market. Warren would be proud.

In this way, dollar-cost averaging really does give you the best of both worlds. You avoid the stress of trying to time the market, and you take advantage of the market's natural ups and downs. It may be simple, but the results are surprisingly powerful.

Take the S&P 500 index over 40 full years, from 1984 to 2024. (See Figure 5.4.) The returns were anything but smooth. In some years, the index surged by more than 30%. In others, it barely moved. And in 2008, during the depths of the global financial crisis, the S&P 500 fell by a staggering 38.49% as the collapse of the US housing market sent shockwaves through the global economy.

Figure 5.4   S&P 500 results by year.

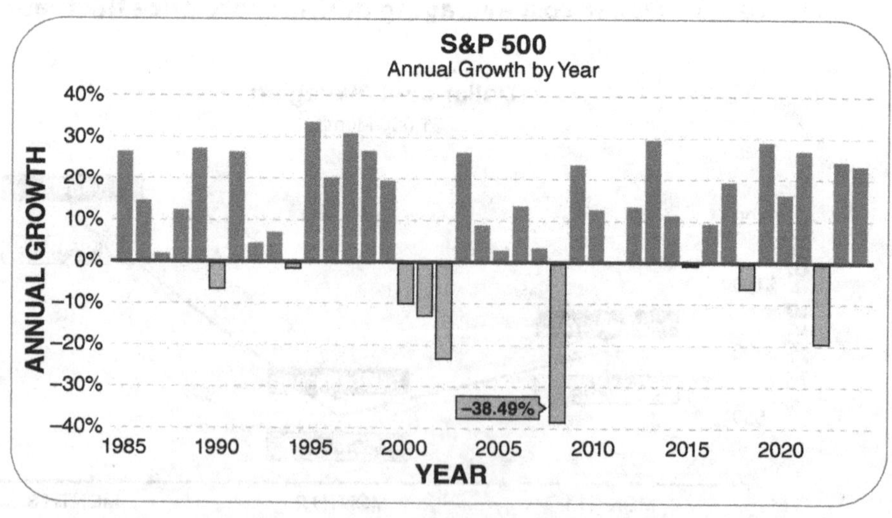

Over that four-decade stretch, investors faced plenty of reasons to panic. There was the Black Monday crash of 1987, the bursting of the dot-com bubble, the September 11 attacks, the great financial crisis, the COVID-19 pandemic, and more recently, surging inflation and sharp interest rate hikes. Each of these events rattled financial markets and tempted investors to pull out.

But what if you had simply stayed the course? If you had invested $5,000 at the end of 1984 and continued investing $5,000 each year until the end of 2024 (without trying to time the market, and without changing your plan), your total contributions of $205,000 would have grown into a portfolio worth more than $2 million.

That is the quiet power of dollar-cost averaging. It rewards consistency, not perfection. And in the long run, staying invested through the noise can make all the difference.

CHOOSING YOUR DOLLAR-COST AVERAGING STRATEGY

Now that you understand how dollar-cost averaging works, the next step is to figure out what your own strategy will look like. This doesn't need to be complicated. In fact, the best approach is usually the one that's simple, realistic, and sustainable over the long term.

Start by asking two basic questions:

1. **How much can I invest?**

   Remember back to Chapter 2, where we analyzed your personal P&L statement? This is where that groundwork becomes useful. Look at your budget and figure out how much you can comfortably invest without ever risking running low on cash. That amount might be $50 a week, $500 a month, or $5,000 a year. Everyone's financial situation is different, so the exact number isn't as important as your ability to stick with it. The key is consistency, through market highs and lows. Even investing just $10 a week adds up over time. Over 40 years, that small habit could grow to around $280,000 (costing you just $20,800 out of pocket).

2. **How often should I invest?**

   The most common approach is monthly, but weekly, fortnightly, or quarterly are also perfectly fine. The best approach is to choose a frequency that matches your income and feels natural. If you're paid weekly, you might invest weekly. If you're a freelancer with irregular income, perhaps you put 10% aside each time you get paid and invest every quarter. The key is finding a system that works for you and committing to regularity.

Once you've answered the two key questions, the rest is remarkably simple, thanks to modern automation. With today's technology, most major brokerage sites allow you to set up automatic transfers from your bank account and even automate the investments themselves. This means your strategy doesn't rely on willpower or constant attention. It runs quietly in the background, building wealth while you focus on everything else.

Brokers like Fidelity, Charles Schwab, Vanguard, Robinhood, E*TRADE, and M1 Finance all offer some version of automated investing. The process typically involves two basic steps:

1. **Setting up automatic transfers** from your bank account to your brokerage account

2. **Automating the regular purchase** of ETF shares based on your schedule

Many brokers today also support fractional share investing, which helps you make the most of every dollar. For instance, if you want to invest $500 but the ETF you've chosen trades at $300 per share, your broker will no longer leave that additional $200 sitting idle. Instead, they'll allocate 1.67 shares to your account, fully investing the entire $500.

If your broker offers these tools, it's well worth taking the time to set them up. Automating your passive investing puts your strategy on autopilot. By handling everything upfront, you remove the friction from the process. There's no need to log in manually, question whether now is the right time to invest, or worry about forgetting during a busy month. Instead, your broker transfers the funds, places the trade, and keeps your plan running smoothly without any extra effort from you.

This is especially powerful for passive investors. After all, the less you interfere, the better. With automation, you're guaranteed not to react to headlines, emotions, or short-term noise. You are just steadily building wealth on autopilot while you focus on the important thing: actually living your life. That sounds pretty good to me.

IMPLEMENTING THE NEW MONEY STRATEGY

As I stressed at the beginning of this book, *The New Money Strategy* is built on four key pillars:

- **Step 1: Get Prepared**
- **Step 2: Lay the Foundation**
- **Step 3: Find Buffett's Bargains**
- **Step 4: Stay the Course**

At this point, we've covered the first two. You've prepared yourself financially and mentally, and you've learned how to lay a rock-solid foundation through passive investing in low-cost ETFs. With a simple strategy like dollar-cost averaging, you now have everything you need to begin building wealth automatically, without relying on market timing or predictions.

Now comes an important decision: how should you structure your overall portfolio?

For most people, a blended approach of passive and active investing makes a lot of sense. In investing speak, this blended approach is called a "core and satellite" approach. Allocating 60–80% of your investable funds to passive investing (your core) provides long-term stability and peace of mind. This portion of your portfolio compounds steadily in the background and requires almost no involvement once it is set up.

The remaining 20–40% can then be used to explore a more active strategy, the same approach used by Warren Buffett and other great investors. This is where you look for high-quality businesses that are trading at discounted prices, with the potential to grow your wealth more aggressively than the broader market. These are the satellites. Of course, this part of your portfolio will take more time and effort, and it carries a little more risk. But for those who enjoy the process and are willing to put in the work, the rewards can be very significant.

Here's a simple way to think about it:

- An **80/20 split** might suit you best if you prefer a mostly hands-off approach with just a small allocation for active investing.
- A **60/40 split** might make more sense if you are eager to study businesses, read financial statements, and search for undervalued opportunities.

That being said, I also want to stress that it is perfectly okay if you decide that passive investing is the only approach you want to follow.

You may already know that you have no interest in researching companies or picking undervalued stocks. You might find the idea stressful or simply unappealing. What you want is a simple, low-maintenance way to invest in the market and build wealth consistently over time. If that's the case, then congratulations. That is exactly what passive investing delivers.

If that sounds like you, I want to reassure you that this is a completely valid choice. I may not personally subscribe to this approach, but it is perfectly valid nonetheless. So here it is, your third option, officially validated via a bullet point and an indent.

- The **100/0 split** where you decide that passive investing is what you feel most comfortable with, and where you want to leave it.

At the end of the day, investing is personal, and the right strategy is always the one you are most likely to stick with. If you feel confident with a 100% passive portfolio, then you already have a plan that works. In that case, you can skip Step 3 of the book and move ahead to Step 4, where we will focus on how to stay committed to your strategy through all types of market conditions.

But if you find yourself curious about the Warren Buffett approach to stock selection, you are not alone. Maybe you have wondered what makes a business truly great. Or how some investors can look at a company and work out "this stock is worth more than the market believes." If that sounds like you, then you are in for an exciting next step.

In Step 3, Find Buffett's Bargains, we build upon our foundation of passive investments and investigate the world of active investing. This is where we begin hunting for the right organizations. You will learn how to think like a business owner, not just a stockholder. We will look at how to identify high-quality companies with durable competitive advantages, how to determine what those companies are worth, and how to buy them at a price that leaves plenty of room for error.

This approach is not about speculation or chasing the latest trends. It is about developing a rational framework for decision-making, built on timeless principles. You will discover how great investors use patience, discipline, and a deep understanding of the businesses they own to achieve outsized returns over time.

So, if you are ready to go beyond autopilot and start applying the same strategies that helped Warren Buffett become one of the most successful investors of all time, then turn the page. Let's begin the search for your first Buffett-style investment.

STEP 3

FIND BUFFETT'S BARGAINS

CHAPTER SIX

FINDING WONDERFUL BUSINESSES

Up until now, we've explored the most common investing strategy in the world today: passive investing. The idea is simple: buy a low-cost, diversified index fund that tracks the market and ride the wave of corporate America over the long haul. You're not trying to beat the market; you are simply participating in the market.

As we discussed in the previous chapter, for many people, that's as far as they want to go. They're not interested in breaking down financial statements, tracking Microsoft's earnings growth, or spending weekends building valuation models. And that's perfectly okay. In fact, it's not just okay; it's recommended. Even Warren Buffett has said that most investors, including LeBron James, would be better off putting their money into a low-cost S&P 500 index fund and leaving it alone.

So, if you've reached this point in the book and realized, "Yep, that's me," then congratulations. Truly. That alone puts you ahead of most people financially, and I wish you all the best on your journey to building long-term wealth.

But if you want to go a step further—if you find yourself curious about how great businesses work, if you enjoy digging into the numbers, and if you see investing not just as a strategy but as a craft—then this next part of the book is for you.

Over the years, even I have found myself gradually moving further away from being a 100% passive investor. Today, about 40% of my invested funds are devoted to active investing in the style of Warren Buffett. At first glance, that might seem counterintuitive. After all, the data show that most active fund managers, whose full-time job is to beat the market, tend to underperform it. So why would I seemingly go against that research?

The short answer is: *multibaggers.*

MULTIBAGGERS AND ACTIVE INVESTING

Multibaggers are the rare businesses that don't just go up 20% or 30%. They double, triple, or even increase 10-fold over time. They're not easy to find, but they do exist. And from what I've learned over the past eight years, uncovering just a handful of these opportunities can significantly transform your long-term returns.

Even Warren Buffett, in one of his recent shareholder letters, admitted:

> In 58 years of Berkshire management, most of my capital-allocation decisions have been no better than so-so … Our satisfactory results have been the product of about a dozen truly good decisions—that would be about one every five years. (Buffett, 2023)

Think about that. The greatest investor of all time, someone who's made hundreds if not thousands of investment decisions, credits the vast majority of Berkshire's success (a staggering 19.9% annual return since 1965) to just a dozen big winners. That's the power of multibaggers.

And that's exactly why I've embraced a Buffett-style active investing approach for a large part of my portfolio. You don't need to get every decision right. In fact, as Peter Lynch once said, you're doing well if you get 6 out of 10 right, and judging by Buffett's track record, it might be even fewer than that. But when you focus on truly great businesses, bought at reasonable prices, and let them run, a few big winners can more than make up for the rest.

Let's put this into perspective.

Say you invest $1,000 today into a low-cost ETF that tracks the S&P 500 and hold it for the next 30 years. Assuming the market's historical average annual return of around 10%, that $1,000 grows into $17,449 by retirement.

Now consider a different approach. You spend the next five years studying, learning, and patiently searching for a truly exceptional business, a potential multibagger. You don't invest a dime during that period. But at the end of those long five years, you finally invest your $1,000 into a company that compounds at 15% annually for the remaining 25 years.

The result? Despite having five fewer years of compounding, your $1,000 investment grows to $32,919. That's 88% more than what you got from the index fund.

That's the power of finding just a few extra percentage points of return. It's the reason Buffett-style investors obsess over quality businesses and are willing to wait patiently for the right opportunity. Because when you find a business that can compound at higher rates for long periods, the payoff isn't marginal. It's life changing.

Over the past eight years, I've found my own multibaggers in companies like Meta, Google, and even Tesla. These select few investments have already grown to the point where they make my passive index holdings look tiny by comparison. But I'm not delusional. I certainly don't think I'm some investing prodigy, and I'd never *assume* I can beat the market forever. And that's exactly why I still keep a solid foundation in passive investments.

However, it's also become clear to me that ignoring active investing altogether would be a mistake. When just a few well-researched decisions can dramatically tilt your long-term results, it makes sense to devote at least a small portion of your portfolio to the Warren Buffett approach. While it's not guaranteed to outperform, not even trying might be the bigger risk.

So, with that said, what is the Warren Buffett method?

Interestingly, I think it was Buffett's long-time business partner, Charlie Munger, who best summed it up. Reflecting on their shared philosophy, Munger once said:

> We have to deal in things that we're capable of understanding. And then once we're over that filter, we have to have a business with some intrinsic characteristics that give it a durable competitive advantage. And then, of course, we would vastly prefer a management in place with a lot of integrity and talent. And finally, no matter how wonderful it is, it's not worth an infinite price, so we have to have a price that makes sense and gives a margin of safety, considering the natural vicissitudes of life.

From that quote, you can extract the four timeless pillars of the Buffett investing approach, which we will obsess over in the coming chapters:

1. **Understand the business**—Only invest in companies you can genuinely grasp.

2. **Look for a durable competitive advantage**—Seek businesses with moats that protect their profits over time.

3. **Assess management**—Prioritize leadership with both integrity and skill.

4. **Buy with a margin of safety**—Even the best business isn't worth any price. You need a rational valuation and a margin for error.

This framework might seem overly simple, but as Munger himself noted, "The reason our ideas haven't spread faster is because they're too simple." Simple, yes, but incredibly powerful. And in the chapters that follow, you'll learn exactly how to apply this strategy with confidence, step by step.

FINDING WONDERFUL COMPANIES

The first step in the Buffett approach is "understanding the business," but before we dive into trying to understand a company, we first need to cover how to find a business to analyze in the first place. There are many publicly traded companies in this world that we could potentially examine. Current estimates are there are approximately 50,000 public companies worldwide, with around 4,000 listed in the United States. But how do we refine this list down to a selection of three or four companies that might be great businesses for us? There is one simple exercise I do, that I first learned from a book called *Rule #1*, written by my investing mentor, Phil Town.

The exercise is all about a pivotal Buffett tenet: staying within your *circle of competence*. The idea is simple: look at companies close to home, within your areas of expertise, interest, and understanding, and never stray into areas you simply cannot comprehend. In his

1996 shareholder letter, Warren Buffett said "The size of your circle of competence is not very important; knowing its boundaries, however, is vital." That's what the following exercise aims to do, keep you firmly inside your own circle.

So, what do we do? Start with a fresh piece of paper. On it write four questions:

1. Where do you spend your time?
2. What do you spend your money on?
3. What are you really good at?
4. What are you passionate about?

Once you've written down those four questions, take your time answering each of them as thoroughly and honestly as you can. This isn't about impressing anyone; it's about identifying real patterns in your daily life. Here's an example of how I answered them when I first did this exercise for myself.

Where do I spend my time?

I spend a lot of time creating content for my YouTube channel, *New Money*, and reading about businesses and investing. In the evenings, I often relax with video games or watch TV shows and documentaries on Netflix, Disney+, and Amazon Prime Video. On weekends, I might catch up with friends, watch sports, or go out for food and drinks. And like most, I'm not immune to the late-night scrolling through social media apps, like Instagram, TikTok, or YouTube.

What do I spend my money on?

I regularly pay for groceries, streaming subscriptions, video games, new tech like camera gear and cell phones, and occasionally I'll buy dinner out. I also buy books on investing and business, and like most people, I have a monthly phone bill and various online services (such as Adobe's Creative Cloud) that I subscribe to.

What am I really good at?

I've built a YouTube channel from scratch, so I know a fair bit about content creation, video editing, and the digital media space. I have a solid understanding of investing and the stock market, and I used to work as a physiotherapist, so I also have some knowledge of healthcare. On top of that, I played Australian football seriously in my teens and still keep up with the AFL today.

What am I passionate about?

I love creating content and educating others about investing. I'm passionate about technology, renewable energy, and the future of transportation (especially electric vehicles). I get excited about well-made video games and spend way too much time following the gaming industry on YouTube. And of course, I love diving deep into company financials and learning how great businesses really work.

Now comes the important part: identifying common themes across your answers. Don't overthink it. Just look for patterns. For me, three themes immediately stood out:

- **Entertainment**—I spend time watching shows and playing games, spend money on it, and I'm passionate about both.
- **Technology and social media**—I create digital content, buy tech gear, use social media on a daily (if not hourly) basis, and follow businesses in the space.
- **Investing and business**—I spend time reading about it, have knowledge in the area, and genuinely enjoy it.

From these themes, I can already start building a short list of industries that fall within my circle of competence. Industries like social media, video games, streaming platforms, digital advertising, and consumer tech. These are spaces I already interact with every day. I naturally understand how they make money, how their products work, and why people use them. That gives me a head start in researching companies in these areas.

Then the final step is simple: Google it. Search for terms like "biggest video game companies," "top streaming platforms listed on the stock exchange," or "publicly traded social media companies." This will give you a real list of businesses to start exploring.

For example, a quick search of "biggest video game companies" brings up names like these:

- **Nintendo** (Mario, Zelda)
- **Microsoft** (Xbox)
- **Sony** (PlayStation)
- **Take-Two Interactive** (Grand Theft Auto, Red Dead Redemption, NBA 2K)
- **Electronic Arts** (FC, Battlefield)

Likewise, searching "largest publicly listed social media companies" turns up the following:

- **Alphabet** (YouTube)
- **Meta Platforms** (Facebook, Instagram, WhatsApp, Messenger)
- **Tencent** (WeChat)
- **Snap Inc.** (Snapchat)
- **Reddit**, **Pinterest**, and more.

Now, to be clear—these are not stock recommendations. Far from it. Most of these companies will be overvalued or unsuitable at various points in time. But that's not the point. The goal is to find businesses you're naturally curious about because they are the ones you're more likely to understand and, therefore, evaluate rationally.

So now it's your turn. Grab a blank page and answer those four questions:

- Where do you spend your time?
- What do you spend your money on?
- What are you really good at?
- What are you passionate about?

Look for themes across your answers. Highlight the industries that appear again and again. Then do a quick search to identify a handful of publicly traded companies in those areas. Your goal isn't to discover "the perfect stock" today. It's to build a shortlist of companies you'd *actually enjoy researching.*

And that's really the secret. I'm a firm believer that you should only look at businesses you find genuinely interesting. Investing is a lifelong endeavor, and if you want to stay engaged for decades, you must enjoy the process. If you're not interested in a company, you'll either stop following it or, worse, invest without enough context. That's how emotional investing mistakes happen.

Even Warren Buffett, arguably the greatest investor of all time, doesn't try to understand everything. He famously keeps a "too hard pile" on his desk, and he's not afraid to use it. If a business is too complicated or he simply isn't interested in learning about it, he moves on. If that approach works for Buffett, it should work for us too.

By sticking to industries you understand (or are interested in understanding), you give yourself an incredible advantage as an investor: focus. Instead of feeling overwhelmed by thousands of options, you narrow your field to a small, manageable group of businesses that actually mean something to you. And with that focus comes depth. My investing mentor Phil Town told me recently that "the important thing about your circle of competence is to go an inch wide and a mile deep," and this couldn't be more accurate. By sticking to companies with relevance to your interests, you won't just be skimming headlines or half-heartedly reading earnings reports. You're genuinely interested. And that means you'll absorb more, notice more, and make better decisions.

But there's an important distinction here. Liking a product is not the same as understanding the business. Just because you use Spotify every day doesn't automatically mean Spotify is a great investment. You still need to understand how the company generates revenue, how profitable it is, what risks it faces, and whether it has a durable edge. That's what defines a real circle of competence. Not just being a fan of the product but being capable of thinking like an owner.

As Charlie Munger once said, "It's remarkable how much long-term advantage people like us have gotten by trying to be consistently not stupid, instead of trying to be very intelligent." The moment you realize something is too complex, too opaque, or just too far outside your wheelhouse, you move it to the "too hard" pile and move on. That discipline is what separates good investors from great ones.

UNDERSTANDING THE BUSINESS: THE ANNUAL REPORT

Now that you've identified a few companies that fall within your circle of competence, it's time to take the first step in the Buffett approach: understanding the business. Before we dive into moats, management, or valuation, we need to focus purely on the foundational elements. That means building a clear mental model of how the business works. In simple terms: how does this company make money, and what are the key moving parts that determine its success or failure?

Until you can answer that question with clarity and confidence, in your own words, you're not ready to invest. Warren Buffett has always said that "you should never invest in a business you don't understand," and for good reason. Without a solid grasp of the underlying mechanics, you'll struggle to spot red flags, assess opportunities, or react rationally when the market gets emotional. In this chapter, we'll break down exactly how to build that understanding so that you can move forward with the rest of your analysis on solid ground.

So where do you begin? One of the best places to start is the company's annual report, also known as the company's *10-K filing*. These documents are freely available online and can be found through the company's investor relations page. The annual reports are the most comprehensive documents companies are required to file, and they are designed to give shareholders a clear overview of the business.

Now, you don't need to read every page cover to cover, and you definitely don't need to understand all the technical accounting jargon. At this stage, your goal is simple: build a clear, big picture understanding of what the business does and how it makes money. Think of it like building a map. You don't need every tiny detail, but you do need to know the main roads and landmarks.

The first section you'll want to focus on is the *Business Description*, that's Part 1, Item 1 of the company's 10-K. It typically appears near the beginning of the report and provides a high-level overview of what the company does, who its customers are, where it operates, and how its business is structured. The goal here isn't to get bogged down in technical detail. Instead, you're looking to answer a simple question in plain English: *How does this company make money?*

Let's use the Walt Disney Company as an example. On the surface, Disney might seem straightforward. Movies and theme parks, right? But in reality, it's an incredibly complex business with thousands of moving parts and multiple revenue streams. Still, by reviewing its business description, we're not trying to memorize every detail. We're simply looking to identify the main roads and landmarks, the key pillars of how the business operates.

Figure 6.1 Disney revenue segments.

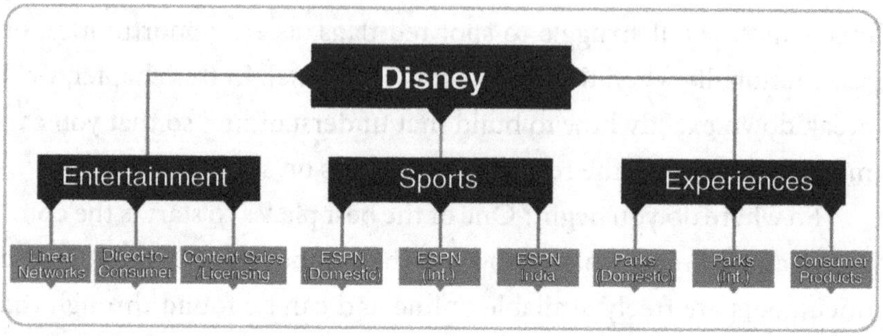

Disney

Entertainment | Sports | Experiences

Linear Networks | Direct-to-Consumer | Content Sales /Licensing | ESPN (Domestic) | ESPN (Int.) | ESPN India | Parks (Domestic) | Parks (Int.) | Consumer Products

In its 2024 annual report, Disney breaks down its operations into three core business segments: Entertainment, Sports, and Experiences. (See Figure 6.1.) Here's how each is described:

1. **Entertainment**—This includes Disney's film and television production and distribution operations, such as Disney+, Hulu, ABC, and theatrical releases. The company says this segment is focused on "creating and delivering branded entertainment content across theatrical, linear and streaming platforms."

2. **Sports**—Driven primarily by ESPN, this segment includes both domestic and international sports networks. Revenue comes from affiliate fees, advertising, and streaming services like ESPN+. According to the company, it "includes the ESPN branded television channels, ESPN+ and Star-branded sports networks."

3. **Experiences**—This is where the magic comes to life physically. It includes Disney's theme parks, cruise line, and resorts, generating revenue from admissions, hotels, food, and merchandise. Disney describes this segment as "creating immersive physical experiences through our parks and resorts around the world." This segment also covers merchandise licensing

for Disney's characters and franchises. Think toys, apparel, books, and more.

(The Walt Disney Company, 2025)

Now, Disney's full business description runs nearly 10,000 words, which is about one-fifth the length of this entire book. And that's not a bad thing. In fact, it's exactly what we want. A great company should be willing and able to explain how it operates in detail. But as investors, we don't need to absorb everything at once. At this early stage, our goal is simply to sketch a rough map. Understand the key segments, how they generate revenue, and what makes the business tick.

Now that we've identified the main segments of Disney's business, the next step is to understand how each segment contributes to the company financially. This means looking at two key figures: revenue and operating income.

Revenue represents the total amount of money a segment brings in before subtracting any expenses. It tells us *how much* business each segment is doing and how much cash is flowing in from customers. It's an indicator of scale.

Operating income, on the other hand, tells us *how profitable* each segment is after deducting the costs of running it. This figure reflects the earnings left over once operating expenses such as staffing, materials, logistics, and administration have been paid. In short, revenue shows you the size, but operating income shows you the strength.

Why does this distinction matter? Because not all revenue is created equal. A segment might generate billions in sales but barely break even once costs are accounted for. Another might bring in less revenue but run so efficiently that it contributes far more to the company's bottom line. As investors, we want to understand both: *which parts of the business are the biggest*, and *which parts are the most profitable*.

So where do we find this information? It should be discussed in Part II, Item 7 of the annual report: Management's Discussion and Analysis of Financial Condition and Results of Operations (commonly abbreviated to MD&A). This section is where the company's management explains, in their own words, the financial performance of the business over the past year. It's one of the most valuable parts of the report because it adds *narrative context* to the raw numbers in the financial statements.

Turning back to Disney's annual report, the report explains the revenue and profit of all three of its segments, but not only that, the report also goes into detail about the revenue and profit of all constituent parts of each segment. See Table 6.1.

With these updated figures, one interesting insight immediately jumps out: while Entertainment brings in the most revenue, it's the Experiences segment that delivers the most profit. In 2024, Disney's Entertainment division generated more than $41 billion in revenue, nearly half the company's total. That makes sense when you consider the scale of Disney+, Hulu, ABC, and their global theatrical releases. But despite all that volume, the segment only produced $3.92 billion in operating income, meaning about 90% of the segment's revenue goes toward covering its costs.

Table 6.1   Disney's Revenue and Operating Income

Segment	Subsegments	Revenue (USD billions)	Operating Income (USD billions)
Entertainment	Disney+, Hulu, ABC, TV & Theatrical releases	$41.19	$3.92
Sports	ESPN, ESPN+, Star-branded networks	$17.62	$2.41
Experiences	Theme Parks, Resorts, Cruise Line, Merchandise	$34.15	$9.27

Meanwhile, the Experiences segment, which includes Disney's theme parks, resorts, cruise line, and merchandise, brought in slightly less revenue at $34.15 billion, yet earned more than double the operating income at $9.27 billion.

This tells us something important: not all of Disney's revenue is created equal. The Entertainment segment may be Disney's most visible business, but it's also capital intensive, competitive, and high cost. By contrast, the Experiences segment, with its pricing power and loyal customer base, runs with far higher margins. As investors, these differences help us understand not just where the money comes from, but which parts of the business are truly driving profitability.

To better understand the business, Disney breaks down revenue and operating income not just by segment but also by subcategory. To see why Experiences is so much more profitable than Entertainment, let's dig into how each segment makes its money. Table 6.2 details Disney's entertainment segment, Table 6.3 shows their sports segment, and Table 6.4 presents their experiences segment.

This breakdown paints a much clearer picture of where Disney's profit truly comes from. In the Entertainment segment, despite pulling in more than $22 billion in revenue from streaming platforms like Disney+ and Hulu, the Direct-to-Consumer business generated

Table 6.2   Disney's Entertainment Segment

Entertainment Subsections	What's Included	Revenue (USD billions)	Operating Income (USD billions)
Linear Networks	ABC, Disney Channel, FX, Nat Geo, A+E Networks	$10.69	$3.45
Direct-to-Consumer	Disney+, Hulu, Hotstar streaming services	$22.78	$0.14
Content Sales/ Licensing and Other	Theatrical releases, TV licensing, home entertainment, music	$7.72	$0.33

Table 6.3 Disney's Sports Segment

Sports Subsections	What's Included	Revenue (USD billions)	Operating Income (USD billions)
ESPN (Domestic)	ESPN TV channels, ESPN+, ESPN on ABC	$15.34	$3.06
ESPN (International)	ESPN channels outside the United States	$1.44	−$0.07
Star India	Star-branded Indian sports channels	$0.84	−$0.64

Table 6.4 Disney's Experiences Segment

Experiences Subsections	What's Included	Revenue (USD billions)	Operating Income (USD billions)
Parks and Experiences (Domestic)	US parks, cruises, resorts, Disney Vacation Club	$23.60	$5.88
Parks and Experiences (International)	International parks and Tokyo Disney licensing	$6.18	$1.35
Consumer Products	Licensing, sale of toys, video games, books, apparel	$4.37	$2.04

just $140 million in operating income. That's a razor-thin margin. In contrast, Linear Networks, with less than half the revenue, brought in over $3.4 billion in profit.

Meanwhile, the Experiences segment continues to shine, particularly the domestic parks business, which contributed nearly $6 billion in operating income on $23.6 billion in revenue. Even Consumer Products, though much smaller in scale, delivered an impressive $2 billion in profit on $4.4 billion in sales.

What this shows is that Disney's legacy businesses (parks, TV networks, and merchandising) are still its financial backbone. Newer ventures like streaming, while massive in scale, continue to struggle with profitability.

UNDERSTANDING THE BUSINESS: THE ONE-PAGER

Now that we've broken down what Disney is and how it makes its money, the next step is to distill that understanding into something simple and actionable: a one-page summary that captures the essence of the business. This is what Warren Buffett refers to as developing a "mental model." It's your own simplified map of the business; how it operates, what drives its performance, where its strengths and weaknesses lie, and what levers management can pull to grow or improve profitability. Writing this out forces you to engage actively with the information rather than passively read it, and it helps solidify your understanding in plain English.

This one-pager will look different for every company, as no two businesses are the same. But at the bare minimum, your page should cover the following:

What the company does (in plain English)
A one-sentence summary of the business model.
e.g., "Disney creates and monetizes entertainment through content, live experiences, and consumer products."

Core business segments
List the company's major divisions or segments.
e.g., Entertainment, Sports, Experiences.

How the company makes money
Bullet points on the main revenue drivers.
e.g., Streaming subscriptions, theme park admissions, merchandise licensing, advertising.

Most profitable segments
Highlight where the real profits come from.
e.g., Experiences generate the highest operating income despite not having the most revenue.

Key strengths/potential competitive advantages
What makes the business hard to compete with?
e.g., Strong brands (Disney, Pixar, Marvel), global theme parks with strong reputation, deep content library.

Key risks or weak spots
What could go wrong?
e.g., Streaming profitability issues, high capital requirements, cyclical park attendance.

Growth levers
What will increase profits or expand the business?
e.g., Improving streaming margins, expanding international parks, upselling experiences.

Then, alongside your written answers, it's also essential to create a simple flow chart of the business. This was one of the most effective tools I used early in my investing journey to truly understand how a company's moving parts fit together. It's one of those things you can sketch out and stick on your wall, and it really helps to cement your understanding of the company. If you find yourself unable to map out how the business works, that's a strong signal it probably belongs in your "too hard" pile. Figure 6.2 shows

Figure 6.2   Disney's flow chart.

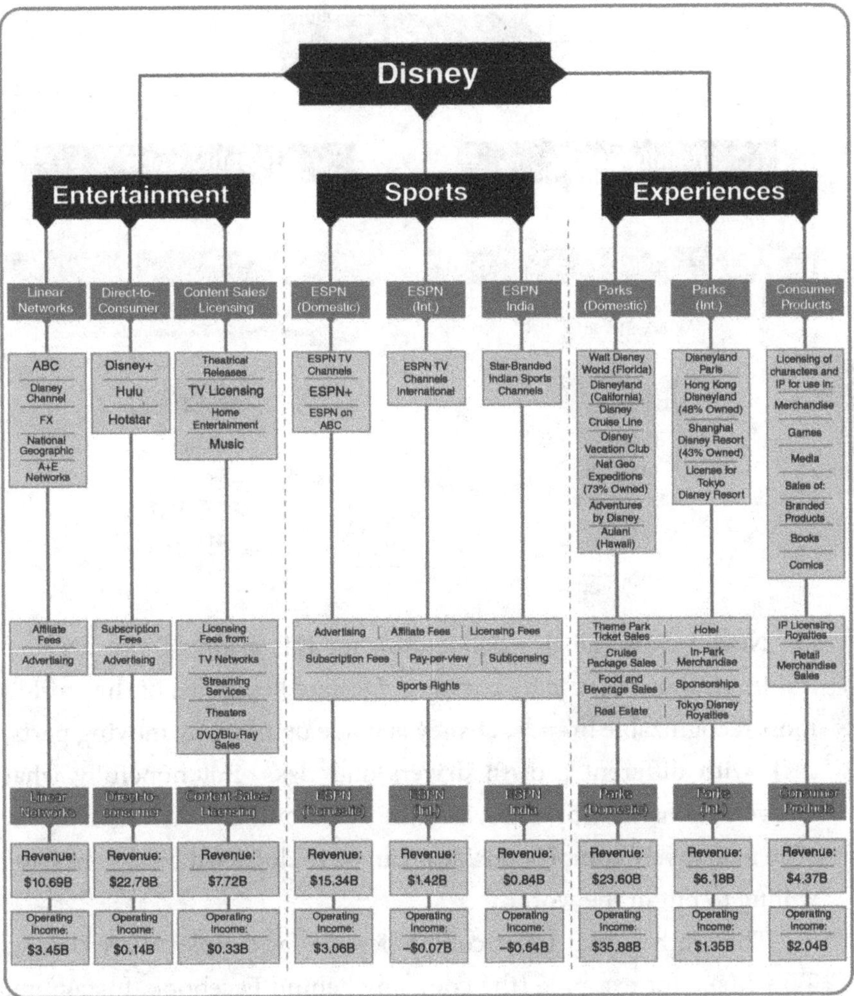

an example of a one-pager I recently sketched after researching Disney. This visual layout helped me clearly see the links between segments, brands, revenue streams, and profitability, making the business far easier to grasp at a glance.

Figure 6.3   Meta's flow chart.

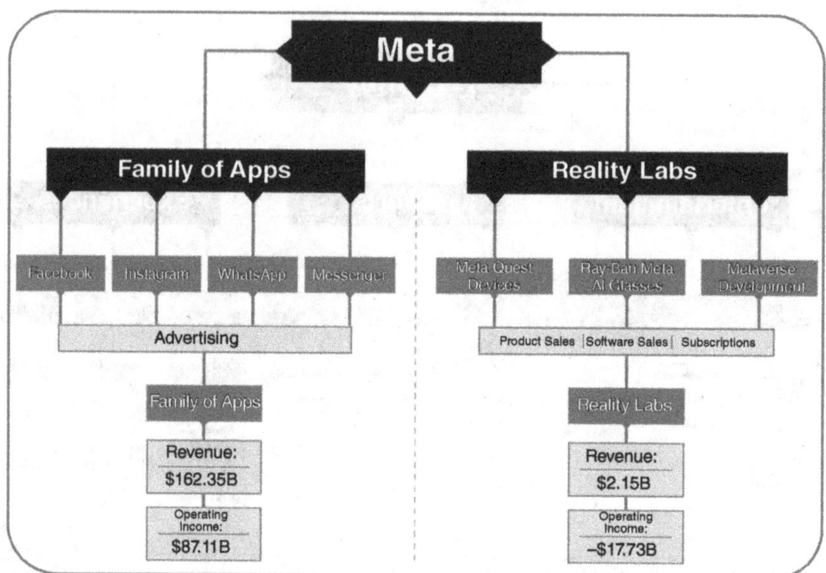

Now, I chose Disney deliberately for this example, not because it's simple, but because it's complex. Despite being one of the world's most recognizable brands, Disney is made up of many moving parts, each with different growth drivers and risks. But hopefully what you've seen is that by following the steps outlined in this chapter, even a relatively complex business can be understood by any investor willing to put in the work.

The truth is that most companies are far simpler than Disney. Take Meta, for example (the company behind Facebook, Instagram, Threads, WhatsApp, and Messenger). Their flow chart is much easier to sketch out, with just a few core apps and one primary way of making money: advertising. See Figure 6.3.

So, if you're finding this process overwhelming, don't panic. Understanding a business doesn't require a finance degree; it just requires curiosity, patience, and a willingness to walk away when things don't click. If you're confused, bored, or feel like you're forcing it, drop the company in your "too hard" pile and go back to the start. Revisit the four questions:

Where do you spend your time?

What do you spend your money on?

What are you really good at?

What are you passionate about?

Pick another company that's closer to your interests and experiences and try again. Once you find a business that's firmly in your wheelhouse *and* you can explain it clearly, then you're ready to take the next step: identifying whether it has a moat.

CHAPTER SEVEN
THE MOAT

When I first heard Warren Buffett—the world's best investor—discussing how water-filled moats protected castles back in medieval times, I thought he'd finally lost the plot. But an hour later, I realized he'd just taught me one of the most valuable investing lessons I'd ever heard.

Back in the Middle Ages, warfare was changing fast. With battering rams, siege towers, and other brutal innovations, castles that let the enemy walk right up to the front gate didn't last long. So, defenders came up with a brilliant solution: the moat. A deep trench, often filled with water, surrounded the castle and turned any attack into a logistical nightmare. Moats slowed down the enemy, funneled them into predictable paths, and gave defenders a huge tactical edge. The wider the moat, the harder it was to breach, and the safer the castle remained.

Buffett's point? The same logic applies to business.

In the business world, a "moat" refers to a company's competitive advantage. It's what protects it from rivals and keeps the profits rolling in. Think about it. There are hundreds of cola brands, but Coca-Cola still dominates. Dozens of smartphones, yet the iPhone consistently leads. Plenty of search engines exist, but we all default to Google. These companies aren't just the lucky ones: they've built moats. Whether it's brand loyalty, network effects, cost advantages, or intellectual property, they possess something that makes them hard to compete with.

It was Warren Buffett himself who first popularized the term *moat* in the world of investing, and he's often said it's one of the most important things he looks for when buying a stock. Back in November 1999, right in the middle of the internet frenzy, Buffett wrote an article in *Fortune Magazine* that stood in stark contrast to the hype around him. At the time, internet stocks were booming, even if the companies behind them weren't making a single dollar in profit. As long as a business had some connection to "the internet," its stock price would skyrocket. To put it in perspective: between 1995 and March 2000, the NASDAQ Composite (an index dominated by tech stocks) soared by approximately 570%. The mania was so extreme that researchers at Purdue University later found that 95 companies that added terms like ".com," ".net," or "internet" to their names saw their share prices jump an average of 74% over the period from five days before the name-change announcement to five days afterward (Lee, 2001). The speculation was egregious. But as we know, the bubble eventually burst. By October 2002, the NASDAQ-100 had collapsed 78% from its peak, and many of the ".com" stocks had filed for bankruptcy.

During the run up, while others were making money by chasing the "hot new thing," Buffett was being criticized for simply sitting tight with investments in more simple businesses like Coca-Cola: companies with strong fundamentals and, most importantly, moats. In that very *Fortune* article (written *before* the crash), Buffett wrote:

> The key to investing is not assessing how much an industry is going to affect society, or how much it will grow, but rather determining the competitive advantage of any given company and, above all, the durability of that advantage. The products or

services that have wide, sustainable moats around them are the ones that deliver rewards to investors. (Buffett, 1999)

Buffett was right. He wasn't just avoiding a bubble; he was teaching a timeless principle: without a moat, any business is vulnerable.

As the dot-com bubble burst and investors lost millions, Buffett marched on, holding every one of his Coca-Cola shares. In fact, he still holds that position today, as the business has continued to flex its powerful moat in the drinks industry over the decades. The result is that his total $1.3 billion dollar investment between 1988 and 1994 is now worth $25 billion today, more than 19 times his original bet. Staggeringly, Coca-Cola's total dividend payment to Berkshire Hathaway in 2024 was $776 million, meaning Buffett is now being paid roughly 60% of his total investment annually in dividends just for going the distance. While this isn't the full story (as one dollar today is worth much less than a dollar in 1988), it still shows a powerful lesson: finding those rare companies with wide moats is a great recipe for investing success.

So, how can we tell if a business we've studied truly has an intrinsic, durable competitive advantage? There are two overarching approaches. First, we assess it qualitatively, by understanding the business model and seeing if it aligns with one of the well-known moats in the business world. Then, we back up our hypothesis with quantitative analysis, specifically, three financial tests that help us measure whether the company's long-term performance actually reflects the presence of a strong moat.

THE QUALITATIVE TEST

Many businesses enjoy competitive advantages that help them stay one step ahead of the pack, and time and time again, it's these strong moat companies that tend to reward shareholders with long-term returns. As we just discussed, Warren Buffett's investment in

Coca-Cola is a classic example of a moat in action. But the Berkshire Hathaway portfolio is packed with other moat-heavy businesses too, from Apple, American Express, and Moody's, to See's Candies, BNSF, and GEICO.

While every business is slightly different, what you'll find is that there are certain types of moats that appear repeatedly across sectors and across markets. So as investors, the first test of a company's moat is a qualitative one. Once we've taken the time to truly understand how the business works, the next step is to ask: Does this company's business model fit into one of the nine classic moat categories?

There's no complex formula or calculator required here. This is a judgment call, using your insight into the business to spot whether it has built-in advantages that give it a durable edge over competitors. It's about recognizing what makes a business hard to compete with and whether that advantage is likely to last. So, with that said, take a look back to the "one-pager" you drew for your company, and see if their business model aligns with any of the following moat types.

Brand Moat

A brand moat is a type of competitive advantage where a company's name and reputation are so strong that customers consistently choose it over competitors, even when similar or cheaper alternatives exist. It allows the company to charge premium prices, maintain customer loyalty, and stand out in a crowded market. This moat is usually built slowly over many years and is typically seen in well-established companies. It's a deeply psychological moat, built on perception, emotion, and trust. And yet, this intangible force can be one of the most powerful assets in business.

A classic example is Apple. Since the release of the iPhone in 2007, Apple has built a reputation for delivering products that are sleek, easy to use, and powerful. From the iPhone to MacBooks to AirPods (all three of which are on my desk as I write this), these products are known as trendy, high-quality products, and the result is that Apple has built a strong reputation. This reputation allows Apple to charge more for their products than their closest competitors and suffer no negative effects to their sales. This premium is commonly referred to as the "Apple tax." On paper a MacBook might have the same technical specifications as the latest Dell laptop, yet somehow, Apple is able to both charge more and outsell Dell's lineup.

Other businesses that often possess brand moats are companies that represent a certain lifestyle, such as Ferrari, Lululemon, Louis Vuitton, or Nike. While companies such as Volkswagen or Toyota manage to pocket 10–20% of their revenue (after subtracting the costs required to manufacture their vehicles), Ferrari keeps approximately 50%. This isn't because Ferrari can build its cars for less; it's because they have figured out that they can sell their vehicles at a far higher premium. But how can Ferrari do this, while Toyota and Volkswagen simply can't? Because the Ferrari badge represents exclusivity and status. Customers are willing to pay big bucks to be a part of that club. A similar effect can be seen in much smaller, cheaper products too. Take shoes for example. I've owned many brands of shoes in my life, and I can guarantee that my Nikes are by no means the most comfortable, durable, or supportive. But as soon as I get dressed to go out with my friends, I reach for my Nike sneakers. So do millions of others around the world. Nike may not make the best shoes, but it doesn't need to. The brand represents a lifestyle, and millions of people want to be part of it. That's the power of a brand moat. It lets companies win not just on product, but on perception.

Switching Moat

 A switching moat is a type of competitive advantage where a company's product or service is so deeply embedded in a customer's life or business that switching to a competitor would be costly, time-consuming, inconvenient, or risky. The "cost" isn't always financial, it can also be about effort, time, retraining, lost data, or disruption to workflow. Because of this, customers are more likely to stay put, even if alternatives exist.

This type of moat is especially common in companies that provide software or systems used by other businesses, particularly when those tools become deeply embedded in day-to-day operations. Take Microsoft Office 365, for example. Businesses have relied on Word, Excel, PowerPoint, and Outlook for decades. These tools aren't just convenient; they're woven into how businesses function. Even if a newer, flashier alternative comes along, most companies won't switch. Why? Because the cost of switching is simply too high. Migrating to a new system would involve transferring data (with the risk of losing it), retraining staff, and dealing with lost productivity during the transition. The potential disruption isn't worth the upgrade, even if the new software is objectively better. As a result, businesses stick with what works, and companies like Microsoft enjoy steady, recurring subscription revenue.

Another powerful example of a switching moat is our previous example, Apple. As the iPhone skyrocketed in popularity, Tim Cook didn't just ride the wave, he doubled down, strategically turning Apple's growing lineup of products into a tightly woven ecosystem. Each new device and service was designed to work seamlessly with the others, making the whole experience smoother, smarter, and more convenient the deeper you go. For example:

- Your MacBook syncs your messages, notes, and photos.
- Your AirPods auto-pair when you open the case.

- Your Apple Watch unlocks your Mac, tracks fitness, and shows notifications.
- iCloud keeps everything in sync across devices.
- You can copy and paste across devices such as iPhone and MacBook.
- Features like AirDrop, Handoff, and FaceTime make the experience feel effortless across devices.

Once you're in, the logic writes itself:

If you have an iPhone, it just makes sense to get a MacBook.

If you have a MacBook, it makes sense to grab AirPods.

And if you're already using all three, why wouldn't your next watch be an Apple Watch?

But here's the key: the more Apple devices you own, the harder it becomes to leave. Switching even *one* product to a competitor means giving up features, breaking workflows, and re-learning systems. It's not just about specs anymore; it's about losing convenience and familiarity. That's the power of Apple's switching moat. It's not a trap; it's a velvet rope. And most customers choose to stay inside.

Network Effects Moat

A network effect is a situation where the more people who use a product or service, the more valuable it becomes to everyone, making it difficult to move away from. It's similar to a switching moat, except instead of costing you time and money, moving away from a network effect usually costs you usefulness or enjoyment. In other words, the value of the product isn't just in the tool itself, it's in who else is using it. The more users, the more utility. The fewer users, the less it's worth. And that dynamic keeps people locked in.

The best examples of network effects can be seen in social media and messaging apps, especially ones like WhatsApp and Messenger, both owned by Mark Zuckerberg's Meta Platforms. Now, let's be real: there's no shortage of ways to message your friends these days—TikTok, Snapchat, Slack, Telegram, Signal, Messenger, WeChat, Discord, WhatsApp, Google Chat ... heck, even email if you're feeling desperate. Okay, admittedly, a few of those might sound like a stretch, but the point is that, technically, the potential options are endless. So, with that in mind, why do more than 2 billion people still choose WhatsApp as their go-to messaging app? It's not necessarily because it has the best features. In fact, most of these apps offer very similar functionality. The reason is simple: everyone else they know is already there.

If your family group chat is on WhatsApp, your friends are on Messenger, and your colleagues use Slack, then that's likely what *you* use too, because switching to something else means losing connection with the people you want to talk to most. If you're reading this within 10 years of the book's release, I'd bet you're still using WhatsApp or Messenger regularly. And I'd also bet it's not your "favorite" app; it's just the one everyone you know uses too. That's the network effect in action: the more people on the platform, the harder it is to leave.

Visa is another company with a network effect. As more people began using Visa cards, merchants couldn't afford to ignore them—they risked losing sales if they didn't. Then, as more merchants started accepting Visa, the value of carrying a Visa card increased for consumers. Shoppers could use their card in more places, which meant less need for cash and a smoother, more convenient experience. This created a flywheel effect.

More *cardholders* ⟶ more *merchants* want to accept Visa

More *merchants* ⟶ more convenience for Visa *cardholders*

This momentum continues to propel Visa forward to this day, and they are now a dominant payment processor globally, along with MasterCard and, to a lesser degree, American Express.

"Secret Sauce" Moat

 Technically, this is called an "intangible assets moat," but personally, I prefer to think of it as the "secret sauce moat." Why? Because it captures the essence of what makes some companies quietly unbeatable.

Businesses with the "secret sauce moat" have powerful advantages that you can't necessarily see or touch, but they give them a huge competitive edge. We're talking about assets that are hard to replicate and even harder to compete with, like the recipe to a fast-food chain's patented "secret sauce." These intangible assets include the following:

- Patents (exclusive rights to game-changing inventions)
- Licenses or government approvals that create legal barriers
- Proprietary tech or trade secrets that no one else can access
- Unique content rights (think Disney owning Marvel or Star Wars)
- Ironclad partnerships or exclusive contracts that lock others out

These "intangible ingredients" are what make the secret sauce moat so delicious. They protect the business, keep competitors at bay, and often allow the company to charge more or operate more efficiently than anyone else. In other words, they don't just have a good product, they've got the recipe no one else can copy.

For example, Pfizer (and other big pharma companies) often have patents on life-saving drugs. When this happens, Pfizer can sell a patented drug like a COVID-19 vaccine or a blockbuster disease treatment without any competition for years. That's the law. This enables them to set high prices and squeeze as much out of their insurmountable competitive position as possible through the duration of the patent. Sure, once the patent expires, generics can enter, but by then, Pfizer's already made its billions.

Another example of a company with the *secret sauce* is Disney; however, its moat comes not from patents, but from iconic intellectual property. Disney owns Marvel, Star Wars, Pixar, and classic characters like Mickey Mouse. No one else can legally use that content. This gives Disney+ an edge, because you can't simply stream *Avengers* or *Star Wars* anywhere else.

Spotify is also exploring the secret sauce moat through exclusive licensing rights. Spotify's multi-million dollar deals with Joe Rogan, Call Her Daddy, and others give them content that you can't find on Apple or YouTube. That kind of exclusivity helps drive subscriptions and user retention.

Finally, a notable company in Warren Buffett's portfolio that has a secret sauce moat is Moody's. Moody's alongside Standard and Poor's (S&P) and Fitch Ratings are the three companies legally recognized to rate bonds and credit in America. Even if a competitor comes along, most institutions only trust or are required to use the big three rating agencies. The result is the US Securities and Exchange Commission has gifted these companies a very wide competitive advantage.

Toll Moat

 A toll moat exists when a company controls critical infrastructure or access points and charges others to use it, regardless of who's on the other side of the transaction. Think of it like owning the only bridge into a busy city. You don't need to build the cars or own the buildings; you just collect

a fee every time someone uses their car to get to a building. Toll moats, as you might expect, are commonly seen in physical infrastructure and have proved to be very reliable generators of recurring revenue. Consider these examples:

- **Railroads:** Railroads own the tracks, and other companies must use them to move freight.
- **Toll Roads and Bridges:** Companies own or operate major highways, tunnels, and bridges, and drivers must pay a toll to use them (sometimes with no alternative route).
- **Pipelines:** Pipeline operators transport oil and gas from producers to refineries or export terminals. These companies charge a fee per volume moved, like a toll on energy.
- **Ports and Shipping Terminals:** Port operators control access to key trade gateways and charge fees for shipping, unloading, and storage.
- **Airports:** Airports own and control critical access points in global travel and logistics. They act as gatekeepers, charging airlines, passengers, and vendors fees to use the facility.

By controlling critical access points—whether it's the movement of freight, commodities, or people—certain companies are able to generate recurring revenue and raise prices incrementally, often without seeing a drop in demand. But toll moats aren't limited to physical infrastructure. Increasingly, we're seeing them emerge in the digital world too.

Thanks to their network effects and near-duopoly, Visa and Mastercard operate as toll collectors on global card payments, taking a small cut of every transaction that runs across their networks. Google charges a toll in the form of advertising, monetizing every internet search that flows through its platform. And perhaps most famously, Apple's App Store acts as a digital toll booth, collecting a 30% commission on app downloads, in-app purchases, and digital subscriptions made on iPhones and iPads. These digital toll moats are just as powerful as their physical counterparts, and often even more scalable.

Cost Advantage Moat

 A cost advantage moat is when a company can produce and sell its products or services at a lower cost than its competitors, without sacrificing quality. This gives it pricing power, better profit margins, or both. In simple terms, these businesses can either charge less and still make money or charge the same and make more than their competitors. This is important in the ruthless arena of business. If you're the lowest cost producer of a no-frills product like PVC pipe, then your competitors can't undercut you. If they do, they're taking a loss, and the longer they do that, the closer they get to bankruptcy. There are four key ways that a company can achieve a cost advantage:

1. **Economies of Scale:** Producing large volumes brings down the per-unit cost
   Example: Walmart buys in massive bulk and passes savings on to customers
2. **Efficient Supply Chains:** Better logistics, sourcing, or production methods
   Example: Amazon's fulfillment network is optimized for speed and cost
3. **Vertical Integration:** Controlling more of the supply chain
   Example: Tesla builds its own batteries to reduce reliance on suppliers and cut out the costs of middlemen
4. **Technological Efficiency:** Using software, automation, or AI to reduce labor and overhead

Example: Domino's Pizza invested in its digital ordering platform, allowing customers to place orders without staff involvement

One of the best examples of a cost advantage moat is Costco, a favorite of the late Charlie Munger. Costco keeps costs down by limiting product selection, embracing no-frills store design, and running on a membership model. Selling a smaller range of products in bulk reduces handling and boosts inventory turnover, its bare-bones stores keep overhead low, and membership fees offset razor-thin margins, allowing Costco to offer low prices without sacrificing profitability. The result? Costco delivers exceptional value to customers while maintaining strong profits, a rare and powerful combination.

Scale Advantage Moat

A scale advantage is seen when a company becomes so large and efficient that its size actually becomes a competitive edge. The bigger it gets, the more it can spread out its costs, negotiate better deals, and operate more efficiently than smaller competitors. Think of it as a business that gets stronger the bigger it grows because its costs per unit drop, its brand gets more recognition, and it gains leverage in the market. For example, as we just mentioned, Walmart is a massive American business that buys and sells in bulk. Because of this size, they are able to squeeze suppliers for better prices, as the suppliers certainly wouldn't want to walk away from that lucrative Walmart contract. Furthermore, its enormous scale allows it to operate on thin margins and still profit, punishing smaller competitors that try to match them.

There are five key benefits of a scale advantage moat:

1. **Lower Costs per Unit:** Big companies can buy in bulk, ship in bulk, and produce at scale, driving down the cost of each item.
2. **Supplier Leverage:** They can negotiate better deals with suppliers because of their buying power. Suppliers want access to large, reliable buyers.
3. **Wider Distribution and Market Reach:** Scale allows companies to reach more customers, more cheaply. They can spend more on marketing, logistics, and infrastructure, and spread those costs over a huge customer base.
4. **Brand Recognition and Trust:** Larger companies are often more trusted simply due to visibility and presence. This further drives volume.
5. **Better Data and Insights:** Bigger businesses often gather more customer data, allowing them to better optimize their processes and improve decision-making.

Another clear example of a scale advantage moat is Amazon's e-commerce business. Over time, Amazon has poured billions into building one of the most advanced logistics networks in the world. With fulfillment centers strategically placed across the globe, heavy investment in robotics and automation, and even its own last-mile delivery fleet, Amazon controls the entire shipping pipeline, something most retailers still outsource to companies like UPS or FedEx. Ultimately, Amazon's scale allows it to ship faster and cheaper than nearly anyone else, giving them a competitive edge that's almost impossible to match.

Barrier-to-entry Moat

A barrier-to-entry moat is closely related to a scale advantage moat, but with a slightly different emphasis. In this case, the focus isn't just on the benefits of being big; it's about the sheer magnitude of investment and infrastructure a company has built over time. The idea is simple: the company has spent so much money, developed such a vast network, and refined its operations to such a degree that for any new competitor to try and replicate it would be financially unrealistic and strategically unwise. In other words, it's not just hard to compete; it's not even worth trying.

Scale Advantage = You're already king of the hill and can see further, move faster, and hit harder.

Barrier to Entry = The hill is so steep and slippery that no one else can climb up in the first place.

Take my parents' favorite type of holiday, cruising, as a real-world example. They love exploring the latest and greatest ships from companies like Royal Caribbean and were especially excited when the company launched "Icon of the Seas," now officially the largest cruise ship in the world. It's an engineering marvel: 1,200 feet long, 20 decks tall, seven swimming pools, six water slides, and room for up to 7,600 passengers. But here's the kicker: this one ship cost $2 billion to build. And it's just 1 of 28 ships in Royal Caribbean's fleet.

As you can imagine, starting a cruise line is very *capital intensive*. You can't just decide to compete one day and throw a boat in the water. The barrier to entry is so high that most companies don't even bother trying. And that's exactly what gives the established players a massive advantage. The industry is so dominated by those who've already built the infrastructure that the top three companies (Royal Caribbean, Carnival, and Norwegian; refer to Figure 7.1) collect around 75% of global cruising revenue (Cruise Market Watch, 2025). In other words, the moat isn't just the size of the ships; it's the size of the investment required to even play the game.

Railroads are another example of a barrier-to-entry moat. Take Berkshire Hathaway–owned Burlington Northern Santa Fe (BNSF), for example. BNSF operates one of the largest freight rail networks

Figure 7.1   Cruise line market share.

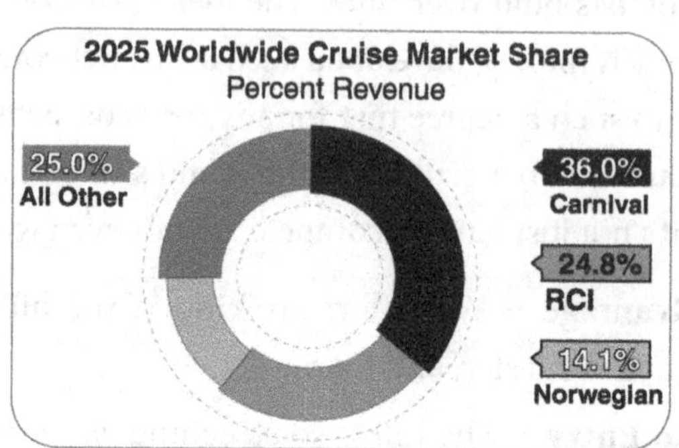

in North America, with over 32,500 miles of track spanning across 28 US states and three Canadian provinces (BNSF Railway, 2025). That infrastructure took decades to build and tens of billions of dollars in capital investment. Now imagine trying to compete with that. You'd need to acquire land, navigate countless regulatory hurdles, secure environmental approvals, and then somehow convince cities and states to let you lay down thousands of miles of new track, all to compete with a company that's already running at massive scale and high efficiency. It's so expensive and complex that no serious competitor has tried to build a new national railroad in decades. And that's the moat: the barrier to entry is so high, it effectively locks out new players. As a result, companies like BNSF operate in an industry with very few competitors, predictable demand, and strong pricing power, making it one of the most stable, defensible businesses around.

Monopoly Moat

Our last moat needs no explanation: the monopoly moat.

You won. You beat capitalism. You're the biggest, the best, and the undisputed champion of your industry. No one even comes close.

Monopolies are the strongest moats in existence because your competitors, uh … don't even exist. There's no price war, no race for market share—you own the market. And as long as regulators stay out of your way, it's about as close to untouchable as a business can get.

Google is a textbook example of a near-monopoly, especially in internet search. Roughly 90% of all global search traffic runs through Google.com, giving it an overwhelming edge in the space (StatCounter Global Stats, 2025). Yes, competitors like Microsoft's Bing technically exist, but with a market share of just 3.95%, they're barely in the conversation. Because so much of the world's search activity flows through Google, the company generates hundreds of billions in ad revenue every year. It's the perfect storm: they've built a massive data advantage, earned global brand trust, and used that dominance and cash flow to expand into a whole ecosystem of products: Chrome, Android, Gmail, Maps, and more. They've also used their strong position to acquire fast-growing platforms, like YouTube, and turn them into even larger parts of the Google universe. The result? A self-reinforcing machine that keeps getting bigger, smarter, and harder to compete with.

It's every investor's dream, but monopolies come with a warning: watch out for the regulators. While investors love monopolies for their pricing power and profit potential, consumers usually hate them. A dominant company can raise prices, reduce choices, and face little pushback, and that's exactly what draws the attention of regulators.

Over the past two decades, as American business has flourished and many industries have consolidated, agencies like the Federal Trade Commission (FTC) and the Department of Justice (DOJ) have stepped up their efforts to rein in monopolistic and anti-competitive behavior.

We've seen major action in recent years:

- In 2020, the DOJ sued Google, accusing it of monopolizing internet search by locking in deals with Apple and Android to see it become their default device search engine.

- In 2022, the FTC went after Meta, claiming it maintained an illegal monopoly in social networking through its acquisitions of Instagram (2012) and WhatsApp (2014).
- In 2022, the FTC challenged Microsoft's $69 billion acquisition of Activision Blizzard, arguing the deal would harm competition in cloud gaming and the console space.

Though the Microsoft–Activision deal ultimately went through, the FTC's lawsuit caught many investors off guard. At the time, the gaming industry appeared highly competitive, with Sony, Nintendo, and Microsoft actively battling for console market share and a wide field of independent publishers and developers thriving across platforms. The FTC's decision to challenge the acquisition signaled a new level of scrutiny, even in markets that didn't look like traditional monopolies. It marked a clear shift toward more aggressive antitrust enforcement, one that continues to this day.

The lesson? Monopolies may print money, but in today's environment, they also paint a big red target on their backs.

Multiple Moats?

While the goal of the qualitative moat test is simply to identify whether a company's business model aligns with at least one classic competitive advantage, it's important to note that some businesses build multiple moats over time, and that's where things get really exciting for investors.

Take Apple, for example. In the 2000s and 2010s, the company built a powerful brand moat through relentless innovation and product design. But over the past decade, Apple has shifted its focus toward building an integrated ecosystem, one filled with features and products that work seamlessly together. This has created a strong switching moat, as moving away from Apple's ecosystem means giving up convenience, functionality, and familiarity.

Apple also exhibits a toll moat, collecting a 30% cut on App Store purchases, subscriptions, and in-app transactions. And when you look at its proprietary technologies (like Face ID and its custom Apple Silicon chips), you start to see signs of a "secret sauce" moat driven by intellectual property and deep technical expertise.

The same applies to Amazon. The company's scale advantage is undeniable, backed by one of the world's most advanced logistics and fulfillment networks. Its network effect keeps growing—the more buyers on the platform, the more sellers are attracted, which in turn draws more buyers. Prime memberships act as a switching moat, locking customers into the Amazon ecosystem. And don't forget the toll moat: Amazon charges third-party sellers fees to access its massive customer base.

Today, many dominant tech companies are protected by multiple moats, and as investors, that's a good thing. The more moats a company has, the harder it is to compete with, and the more secure its profits are likely to be.

So now it's your turn. The first step to uncovering a moat is to take these nine common competitive advantages and see if they match up with the core characteristics of your chosen business. Hopefully the answer is obvious, and as Mohnish Pabrai says, "it whacks you over the head with a 2 × 4." But if it's not quite clicking yet, never fear. We're only halfway there. The next step is to dive into the numbers and examine whether our hypothesized moat is confirmed by the numbers.

CHAPTER EIGHT

THE THREE MOAT TESTS

Once you've spotted the qualitative signs of a competitive advantage, the next step is to see if the numbers confirm the story. A moat isn't real unless it shows up in the financials. That's why in this chapter we'll run through three stress tests—practical, time-tested checks that investors around the world use to separate enduring businesses from those that only *look* impressive.

Following are the three moat stress tests:

1. The Standout Test
2. The Two Engine Test
3. The Capital Efficiency Test

Now, I must admit, this part does involve a bit of math, but don't worry, an eighth grader could do this. Just think of these tests as quick mathematical checks to help confirm whether the company's competitive edge shows up in the financial results.

It's also important to remember that moats don't always look the same, especially across different industries. For example, a capital-intensive business like Berkshire Hathaway's BNSF Railway may struggle to maintain a high return on invested capital (explained in the Capital Efficiency Test) due to the sheer scale of infrastructure involved. But that doesn't mean it lacks a moat; quite the opposite. In BNSF's case, its moat is built around massive barriers to entry.

So, while these tests are incredibly useful, they aren't absolute. Passing all three isn't necessarily a requirement, but if a company does, chances are you've found a business with a serious advantage over its competition.

THE STANDOUT TEST

The Standout Test is exactly what it sounds like: we're looking for a business that clearly rises above the pack. Specifically, we focus on the company's *gross margin* to see whether it can consistently charge more for its products or services than its competitors. A higher gross margin often points to pricing power, brand strength, or a cost advantage, all of which are classic signs of a moat. If a company stands out here, it's worth a closer look.

What is "gross margin"?

Gross margin is a measure of how much money a company keeps after covering the direct costs of producing its goods or services. In simple terms, it tells you how profitable the core product/service is, before accounting for overhead like rent, marketing, or administration costs.

Let's use the classic lemonade stand as an example.

Imagine it costs you $2 in materials (lemons, sugar, water, and a cup), and $1 in labor to make each cup of lemonade. That's $3 in direct costs per cup.

If you sell each cup for $5, you make $2 in gross profit. Your gross margin is simply the percentage of your revenue that you get to keep. In this case, 40%.

$$\text{Gross Margin} = \frac{\$2}{\$5} = 40\%$$

Gross margin tells you how efficiently a company makes money from its core operations, but it does not factor in things like office expenses, research and development salaries, rent, marketing, or taxes. It only considers the direct costs of producing the end product.

For example, Google might sell a smartphone for $1,000, but if it costs $800 to make (materials, assembly, shipping, etc.), the company's gross margin is only 20%. However, if Google was able to reduce its costs to $600, the gross margin would jump to 40%. Even better, if it was able to both reduce costs to $600 per smartphone and raise the sale price to $1,200, the company's gross margin would rise to 50%. In that instance, for every $1 in smartphone *revenue* generated, you're keeping $0.50 after covering your direct costs.

$$\text{Gross Margin}(\%) = \frac{\text{Revenue} - \text{Cost of Goods Sold}}{\text{Revenue}} \times 100$$

In the financial statements, "gross margin" is applied to the entire company rather than an individual product line, but the same formula applies. To calculate a company's gross margin, you will need to look at the income statement. For example, in 2024, Google's parent company, "Alphabet," reported $350.02 billion in revenue and had $146.31 billion of direct costs (cost of revenue) (Alphabet Inc., 2024). Using the following equation, we can see this gave Alphabet a gross margin of 58.20%.

$$\text{Gross Margin(\%)} = \frac{\text{Revenue} - \text{Cost of Goods Sold}}{\text{Revenue}} \times 100$$

$$= \frac{350.02 - 146.31}{350.02} \times 100$$

$$= 58.20\%$$

Compare this to a company such as Walmart. In its 2024 Annual Report, Walmart reported *revenue* of $674.54 billion and *cost of revenue* of $511.75 billion (Walmart Inc., 2025).

$$\text{Gross Margin(\%)} = \frac{\text{Revenue} - \text{Cost of Goods Sold}}{\text{Revenue}} \times 100$$

$$= \frac{674.54 - 511.75}{674.54} \times 100$$

$$= 24.13\%$$

But does that mean Alphabet has a stronger moat than Walmart? Not necessarily, because they operate in completely different industries with very different business models. When analyzing a company's gross margin as a clue to its moat, the key is to compare it to others **within the same industry**. You're looking at the business and its peers and asking, "Does this company stand out from the crowd?"

If a business consistently posts significantly higher gross margins than its peers, that's a strong signal it has pricing power, cost efficiency, or both. These are the hallmarks of a potential competitive advantage.

Imagine we were studying Ferrari as a potential investment opportunity. There are many automakers out there, from luxury manufacturers like Ferrari and BMW, to your daily drivers like Toyota or Honda. Figure 8.1 compares Ferrari alongside the 10 largest automakers in the world (some luxury, some not). Table 8.1 shows how they all stack up when considering their 2024 *gross margin*.

As you can see, one of these is not like the others. Ferrari clearly stands out with a gross margin of 50%.

This means Ferrari can sell its cars for *double* what it costs to make them. But unlike traditional automakers, this margin isn't

Figure 8.1   Graph of automaker's gross margins.

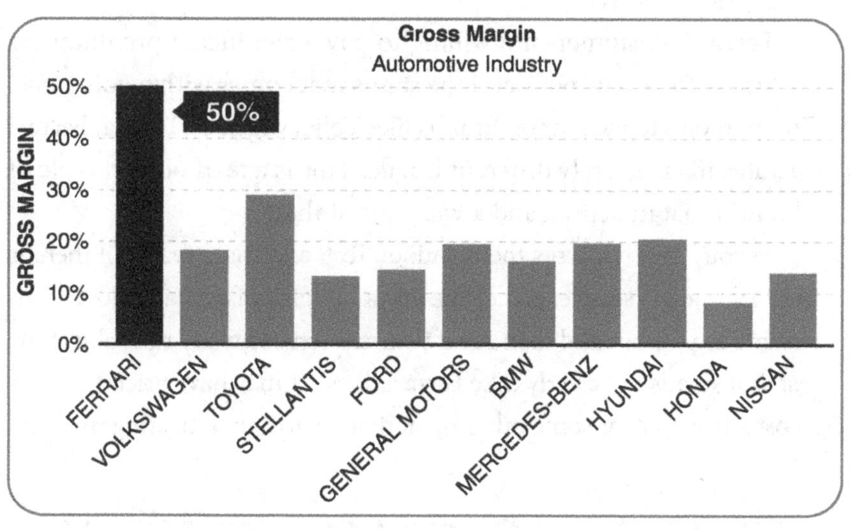

Table 8.1   Automaker's Gross Margins

Company	Gross Margin (%)
Ferrari	50.13
Volkswagen	18.32
Toyota	28.95
Stellantis	13.08
Ford	14.36
General Motors	19.41
BMW	16.10
Mercedes-Benz	19.63
Hyundai	20.40
Honda	8.14
Nissan	13.88

driven by cost-cutting or manufacturing efficiency; it's driven by sheer pricing power.

Ferrari's customers are willing to pay a significant premium for the brand, the exclusivity, and the status that comes with owning one. Compared to mass-market brands like Volkswagen or Toyota, Ferrari operates in an entirely different league. This is a textbook example of a brand moat in action, and a wide one at that.

Ferrari clearly passes the Standout Test, and that's really all there is to it. Your job is simple: gather the gross margins of as many close competitors as you can and then see if your chosen company rises above the rest. If it stands out clearly (like Ferrari does), it may have pricing power, a cost advantage, or some other moat that's worth investigating further.

THE TWO ENGINE TEST

Think of a passenger plane. Sitting on the tarmac, it is nothing special, just a giant hunk of metal taking up space. But once it roars down the runway and lifts into the air, it transforms into something extraordinary: a flying bus that can carry people anywhere in the world in comfort.

What makes that transformation possible? Its engines. Without both firing at full strength, the plane never leaves the ground.

Our business is the same. When the company's *growth* and *profitability* engines are running at full power, that's when it too can launch into the sky.

To look at both growth and profitability for this test, we assess *revenue* and *operating margin* over time, looking for strong growth in both metrics.

- Remember that revenue is simply the total amount of money a business brings in from selling its products or services. It's every dollar a customer hands over before the company pays any bills.

- Example: If a pizza shop sells 1,000 pizzas at $10 each, its revenue is $10,000. That's just sales, not profit.
- Operating margin on the other hand tells you how much profit a company keeps from its revenue after paying for the costs of running the business. It's like saying: "Out of every $1 in revenue, how much does the company keep after covering its rent, staff, supplies, etc.?"
  - Example: If the pizza shop earns $2,000 in operating income from $10,000 in revenue, its operating margin is 20%. That means it keeps 20 cents of profit for every dollar it earns, before taxes and interest.
- Note that "operating margin" is different from "gross margin" that we used in the Standout Test. Gross margin is what's left after considering only the *direct* costs of making the product, whereas operating margin also subtracts *indirect* costs, such as research and development, sales and marketing, and administrative staff.

If a company is consistently growing its revenue year after year *and* improving its profit margins over that same period, it suggests the company is pulling away from competitors, not just growing with the market. This combination can signal the presence of a competitive advantage that is allowing the business to scale efficiently.

Why is this such a strong moat signal? In the real world, growing a business often comes at a cost. Companies typically face a balancing act between two goals: growing revenue and improving margins. Here's the trade-off:

1. **Grow Revenue → Operating Margins Often Fall**

   To attract new customers, expand into new markets, or gain market share, companies often need to lower prices, increase advertising spend, or invest heavily in new products and infrastructure. These strategies can successfully boost sales, but they often eat into profit margins, meaning the business is making more sales, but keeping less profit from each dollar earned.

2. **Improve Margins → Revenue Often Slows**
   On the other hand, when companies focus on improving their margins, it often means cutting back. They might raise prices, reduce staff, cut down on marketing, or eliminate unprofitable segments of the business. These moves can increase profitability, but they tend to slow down growth. Customers may push back on price hikes, and a lack of investment can cause innovation and customer acquisition to stall. In other words, the business becomes more efficient, but not necessarily bigger.

That's why it's so impressive when a company manages to grow its revenue *and* expand its profit margins at the same time. It suggests that the business has a real competitive advantage. These businesses have found the secret to not only make more sales each year, but to keep more from every sale they make. Companies that can do this are usually benefiting from things like brand loyalty, network effects, switching costs, or economies of scale. They're not just growing; they're getting stronger as they grow. This is rare, and when you see it, it should grab your attention. It often means you're looking at a business with pricing power and a moat that may be widening over time.

So, what exactly are we looking for in the Two Engine Test?

To pass, a business needs to demonstrate that it's not just growing, but it's becoming more profitable as it grows. You guessed it—this means both engines are firing.

Start by checking for consistent revenue growth, ideally at 10% per year over the past 10 years. This shows the business is expanding at a healthy pace. Then, look at the operating margin. At the very least, it should be holding steady, but ideally, you want to see it improving over time. That's a strong signal the company is scaling efficiently and could be benefiting from a moat.

Let's look at a company such as Microsoft. Qualitatively, they have a very strong switching moat, but does that hold up when looking at the Two Engine Test?

1. Revenue Growth

Table 8.2 shows how Microsoft's revenue has grown from 2015 to 2024.

Over the past 10 years, Microsoft has grown its revenue from $93.58 billion in 2015 to $261.80 billion recorded in the last 12 months. This means its revenue has grown at a compound annual growth rate of 10.84%, showing that Microsoft's first engine is firing well. But what about the other? Has its operating margin been improving over time?

When calculating the compound annual growth rate, I simply search "CAGR calculator" on Google. Plenty of free websites are available—all you need to do is plug in the initial value (in this case $93.58 billion), the end value ($261.80 billion), and the number of years (10). This will give you the compound annual growth rate of 10.84%.

2. Operating Margin

Table 8.3 shows Microsoft's operating margin from 2015 to 2024.

As you can see from Table 8.3, in 2015 Microsoft generated $93.58 billion in revenue and kept $28.17 billion as operating profit, resulting in an operating margin of 30.10%. That alone is impressive, but what's even more remarkable is how that margin has improved over time. In just 10 years, it has grown from 30.10% to 44.96%, a significant leap of nearly 15 percentage points.

This performance shows that Microsoft's growth and profitability engines are both running at full power. The company has increased

Table 8.2   Microsoft Revenue (Past 10 Years)

Year	2015	2016	2017	2018	2019	2020	2021	2022	2023	2024	TTM
Revenue ($M)	93,580	91,154	96,571	110,360	125,843	143,015	168,088	198,270	211,915	245,122	261,802

Source: Adapted from Seeking Alpha., (2025)

Table 8.3   Microsoft Operating Margin (Past 10 Years)

Year	2015	2016	2017	2018	2019	2020	2021	2022	2023	2024	TTM
Revenue ($M)	93,580	91,154	96,571	110,360	125,843	143,015	168,088	198,270	211,915	245,122	261,802
Operating Income ($M)	28,172	27,188	29,331	35,058	42,959	52,959	69,916	83,383	88,675	109,433	117,711
Operating Margin (%)	30.10	29.83	30.37	31.77	34.14	37.03	41.59	42.06	41.84	44.64	44.96

Source: Adapted from Seeking Alpha., (2025)

its revenue at a compound annual growth rate of more than 10% across the past 10 years, and it has done so while steadily *improving* its margins.

That's a strong sign of a competitive advantage. It suggests that not only are more customers choosing Microsoft, but they're also willing to pay more for its products. Alternatively, it may reflect the company's ability to improve efficiency and reduce costs without losing customers. Either way, it points to a business that is becoming stronger over time and distancing itself from the competition.

THE CAPITAL EFFICIENCY TEST

Finally, we have the Capital Efficiency Test. This is where we test how good a company is at investing in itself. When a company has a moat, it should be able to invest in itself and consistently earn above-average returns on that invested capital because it doesn't face intense competitive pressure. *Return on invested capital* (ROIC) is a metric that tells us whether the company in question has been able to do just that. In short, this number shows us how effectively a company can use its money to make more money.

More specifically, it measures how much profit a business earns for every dollar it invests into the business, like building factories, buying equipment, or expanding operations. A high ROIC means the business has something going for it, whereas a business with a low ROIC shows it needs to invest lots of money to achieve only minimal returns.

To explain this one, I'm taking a stroll down memory lane to my very first job—mowing my neighbor's lawns.

Little Brandon has been saving up his Christmas money from Grandma and Grandpa and Oma and Opa (thanks to his Dutch heritage), and he decides to invest some of that money into getting a lawn care business off the ground. He makes the following purchases:

1.	Lawn mower	$300
2.	Initial fuel	$40
3.	Flyers and advertising	$20

In this instance, Brandon's total invested capital is $360. At the end of the summer, Brandon mows 50 lawns at $25 each.

$$\text{Revenue} = 50 \times \$25$$
$$= \$1{,}250$$

Over the summer, Brandon's operating costs (gas, small equipment fixes, etc.) total $250.

To calculate the ROIC, we first calculate operating profit (after taxes) and then divide this amount by our invested capital.

$$\text{ROIC} = \frac{\text{Net Operating Profit After Tax}}{\text{Invested Capital}}$$

For Brandon's lawn care business, his operating profit is the $1,250 of revenue he made from mowing 50 lawns, minus the $250 of operating costs he incurred over the summer.

$$\text{Operating Profit} = \$1{,}250 - \$250$$
$$= \$1{,}000$$

For this example, as little Brandon is still a kid, we're going to assume he pays no tax and therefore his "operating profit" is also his "net operating profit after tax (NOPAT)." Then finally, to calculate the return on invested capital, simply divide the NOPAT by Brandon's invested capital (the original $360 invest to get the business up and running).

$$\text{ROIC} = \$1{,}000 \div \$360$$
$$= 278\%$$

That means for every $1 Brandon invested in the business, he's earning $2.78 in after-tax operating profit. That's an incredibly high return, and likely a sign of a strong moat if it's sustainable over time.

When analyzing large corporations, I will admit, the numbers may look more daunting, but remember, the same basic formula applies. ROIC is simply NOPAT divided by the company's invested capital.

$$\text{ROIC} = \frac{\text{Net Operating Profit After Tax}}{\text{Invested Capital}}$$

where

$$\text{NOPAT} = \text{Operating Income} \times (1 - \text{Effective Tax Rate})$$

and

$$\text{Invested Capital} = \text{Equity} + \text{Total Debt}$$

In this calculation, operating income is found midway down the *income statement*, the effective tax rate can usually be found by word searching on a company's annual report, shareholder equity is found toward the bottom of a company's *balance sheet*, and total debt is found by adding a company's short- and long-term debt (found as liabilities on the business's *balance sheet*). It is also worth noting that should a business fail to include its effective tax rate, this can also be calculated by dividing a company's tax expense by its income before provision for income taxes (EBT).

Let's use Google (Alphabet Inc.) as an example.

In 2024, the company posted the following:

- Operating income: $112.39 billion
- Effective tax rate: 16.4%

- Shareholders' equity: $325.08 billion
- Total debt: $11.88 billion

(Alphabet Inc., 2024)

$$\text{Alphabet ROIC} = \frac{112.39 \times (1 - 0.164)}{325.08 + 11.88}$$
$$= 27.9\%$$

What does that mean? Google earned a 27.9% return on the capital invested in the business. This is an exceptionally strong number and a key indicator of a wide and durable moat. For every $1 of capital invested into Alphabet's operations, the company generated $0.28 in profit, after tax.

That kind of return doesn't happen by accident. It reflects a business with the following attributes:

- Strong pricing power (thanks to Google Ads)
- Low capital needs (as a digital platform)
- A dominant market position with network effects and data advantages

What about another business, without these same advantages? Take a company such as AT&T, a telecommunications provider nestled in a competitive environment with high capital needs. In its 2024 annual report, the company posted the following:

- Operating income: $19.05 billion
- Effective tax rate: 26.6%
- Shareholders' equity: $118.25 billion
- Total debt: $123.53 billion

(AT&T Inc., 2024)

$$\text{AT\&T ROIC} = \frac{19.05 \times (1 - 0.266)}{118.25 + 123.53}$$
$$= \frac{13.986}{241.78}$$
$$= 5.8\%$$

AT&T's return on invested capital is reasonably low, roughly 6%, meaning it generates ~$0.06 in profit for every $1 of capital invested. This is a sign of

- a capital-intensive business (like telecommunications),
- heavy debt and infrastructure costs,
- and possibly low pricing power or intense competition.

Overall, Google and AT&T are two very different businesses in two very different industries, but these examples go to show just how much variance there can be in ROIC results. But how do we know what's a good ROIC and what's less than impressive?

While there's no absolute right or wrong, Table 8.4 shows a general rule of thumb that many investors use.

When a company consistently earns 15% or more on invested capital, that's when Buffett-style investors start paying attention. Why? Because it means that every $1 the company reinvests in itself is producing $0.15 or more in profit, after taxes.

As we saw with Google's ROIC of 27.9%, there's clearly something special going on. That kind of return doesn't just happen in a competitive market. For Google to generate nearly 28 cents of after-tax profit for every dollar it reinvests, it's a strong signal that the business has a durable moat keeping competitors at bay.

But here's the catch: *one good year isn't enough to confirm a moat.*

Sure, Google posted an impressive ROIC in 2024, but was it a fluke?

Table 8.4   ROIC Ranges

ROIC Range	What It Means
15% or higher	Excellent—likely indicates a moat
10%–15%	Solid—respectable returns
Below 10%	Weak—probably no competitive edge

To gain real confidence in a company's competitive edge, we need to look at trends over time, not just a single data point. That means examining ROIC over the past 10 years to see whether the business has been consistently efficient with its capital.

For instance, if a company posted a 12% ROIC last year, but that's declined from 40% a decade ago, it's a clear red flag that its moat may be eroding. A declining ROIC over time could mean competition is intensifying, pricing power is fading, or operational efficiency is slipping. These can all be signs that the castle walls are being breached.

Let's look at how Google's ROIC has performed over time. Table 8.5 shows the specific percentage of ROIC, and Figure 8.2 provides a bar chart for a more visual comparison.

While some year-to-year fluctuations are natural, the overall ROIC trend is unmistakably upward, rising from 13% in 2015 to 28% in 2024. That kind of long-term improvement is a powerful signal that this business likely has a durable competitive advantage.

Not only is Google's ROIC consistently above the 15% threshold that often points to a moat, but the fact that it's rising over time

Table 8.5   Google ROIC (Past 10 Years)

Year	ROIC (%)
2015	13
2016	13
2017	9
2018	16
2019	15
2020	15
2021	25
2022	23
2023	25
2024	28

Figure 8.2   Graph of Google's ROIC (past 10 years).

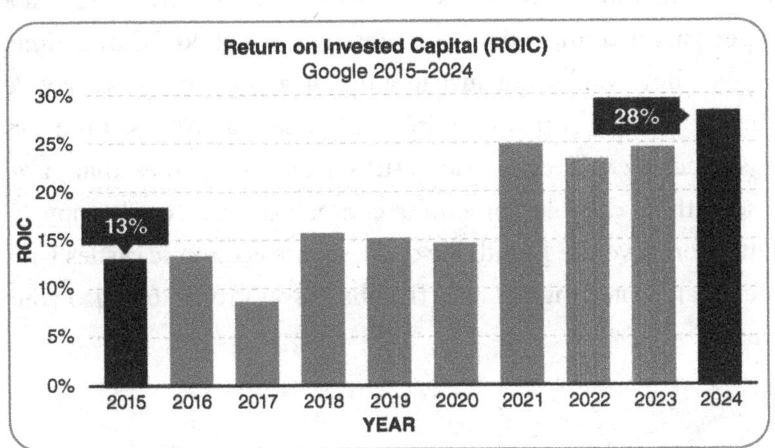

suggests something even more impressive: the company is getting better at reinvesting its capital. In other words, year after year, Google's management is finding ways to deploy each dollar into increasingly profitable opportunities, a hallmark of elite capital allocators and a widening moat.

PUTTING IT INTO ACTION

Now that you've learned both the qualitative and quantitative approaches to moat analysis, it's time to put them into practice. Start with a business you're genuinely interested in. First, ask yourself whether you can spot a moat based on the story, such as the products, the brand, or the network effects. Then, run it through the stress tests in this chapter to see if the numbers confirm your hunch.

At the 1995 Berkshire Hathaway Shareholder Meeting, Warren Buffett famously said, "In business, I look for economic castles protected by unbreachable moats." That's exactly what the three stress tests are designed to help you uncover. If a company has a standout gross margin, a long-term track record of growing both its revenue and operating margin, and it has maintained a high ROIC over time, then you know you're not just looking at a good business, you're looking at a well-fortified one. In reality, these aren't just numbers on a spreadsheet. They're real results from companies that have built something durable, something competitors can't easily copy. In Buffett's words, you've found one of those rare economic castles with a wide moat, protecting not only the businesses profits, but also your returns.

CHAPTER NINE

ASSESSING MANAGEMENT'S INTEGRITY

When we own portions of outstanding businesses with outstanding managements, our favorite holding period is forever.

> – Warren Buffett, 1988 Berkshire Hathaway
> Shareholder Letter

When analyzing companies, Buffett-style investors spend a lot of time evaluating the business model and identifying whether the company has a durable competitive advantage, a "moat." And rightly so. But that only gets you halfway to what Warren Buffett would describe as a truly "wonderful business."

Sure, a moat protects the business from competition, but equally, one of the most important drivers of long-term success is the quality of the people steering the ship. The decisions made by the management team (especially the CEO) can make or break shareholder returns. That's why investors should look for leaders who think like owners, act with integrity, and are focused on creating long-term value.

It's true that a strong business model can carry a lot of the weight. As Buffett famously quipped, "I try to buy stock in businesses that are so wonderful that an idiot can run them. Because sooner or later, one will." In other words, a great company can survive poor leadership for a while. But when you pair a strong moat with a smart, honest, and investor-aligned management team, you dramatically increase your chances of long-term investing success.

THE ORGANIZATION'S LEADERS

When it comes to company leadership, there are plenty of important roles. Chief financial officers (CFOs) manage the money, chief operations officers (COOs) oversee day-to-day operations, and chief technical officers (CTOs) drive the company's technology and innovation. But none carry as much weight as the CEO, the chief executive officer.

The CEO is the face and voice of the company. Think of Bill Gates (and now Satya Nadella) at Microsoft, Steve Jobs (and now Tim Cook) at Apple, or Elon Musk at Tesla or SpaceX. These leaders aren't just symbolic figureheads; they're the ones making the big calls, setting the direction, and shaping the culture of the entire organization. Because of this, the CEO should have the deepest understanding of the business, a strong work ethic, and ideally, skin in the game, meaning they own shares and care about the long-term value of the company (just like you do). They often earn the highest salary, but that compensation should come with accountability and alignment with shareholder interests.

From here, our focus is going to be on the CEO. More than any other executive, they can make or break a business. When you're investing for the long term, the person at the top matters, often more than people realize.

My good friend Hamish Hodder once told me that when he assesses management (especially the CEO), he's really just evaluating two core traits:

- **Integrity:** Is this person honest, transparent, and trustworthy? Do they communicate openly with shareholders, admit mistakes, and put the long-term health of the business ahead of short-term pressures?
- **Talent:** Do they have the skill, vision, and discipline to grow the business, allocate capital wisely, and navigate challenges? Can they lead the company strategically and make decisions that build long-term value?

That simple idea has stuck with me ever since. It perfectly captures what we should look for in a great leader. As shareholders, we're not just investing in a business; we're placing our trust in the person running it. A strong CEO needs to be honest and transparent, even when things aren't going well. But integrity alone isn't enough. They also need to show they have the skill and vision to steer the company in the right direction, make smart capital allocation decisions, and build long-term value. In short, we want someone who treats the company like an owner, not just an employee.

But then comes the next question: how do we actually assess integrity and talent? These are intangible qualities, but they leave very real clues in a CEO's actions, decisions, and communication.

In each case, there are a few key tests you can use to check whether a CEO is truly acting in the best interests of shareholders. In the next chapter, we'll get into assessing a CEO's talent, but for the rest of this chapter, we'll explore assessing a CEO's integrity.

ASSESSING INTEGRITY

In a 1998 lecture at the University of Florida, Warren Buffett said, "In looking for people to hire, you look for three qualities: integrity, intelligence, and energy. And if they don't have the first, the other two will kill you." It's a powerful quote, and while he was talking about hiring, the exact same logic applies when evaluating the CEO of a company you're investing in.

The first step in assessing a company's leadership is asking one simple question: Does the CEO consistently act with integrity? Unfortunately, I learned this lesson the hard way.

One of my biggest investing mistakes came from putting too much faith in a CEO who didn't deserve it. The company was an Australian-listed business aiming to build a global network of telecommunication nanosatellites. The vision sounded incredible, similar in ambition to what SpaceX's "Starlink" has become today. They even managed to get a few test satellites into orbit to prove the concept worked.

But behind the scenes, cracks were forming. Timelines kept slipping, funding kept running dry, and shareholder updates began to sound more like excuses than transparency. Looking back, I was too naive to see the signs. I wanted to believe the story, and I put my trust in the CEO's words rather than the company's actions.

In 2020, the company entered voluntary administration after failing to secure the funding it needed. The ambitious dream collapsed, and I was left with a harsh but valuable lesson: no matter how exciting a company's vision is, if management lacks integrity, it's only a matter of time before reality catches up.

Since that moment I vowed to always scrutinize the CEO's integrity. If the CEO sounds as though they aren't being open and honest, there's no way to know for sure that they aren't hiding important information from the shareholders. For this reason, there are two key steps I always take in assessing the CEO's integrity: watching how they communicate and watching how they are paid.

Watch How CEOs Communicate

One of the most revealing ways to assess a CEO's integrity is by observing how they communicate, especially during challenging times. As shareholders, we have the right to clear, honest updates from the people running the company, and CEOs are expected to deliver that transparency through a few key channels:

- **Annual Shareholder Letters:** Typically attached to the company's annual report, this is where the CEO reflects on the past year, highlights wins and losses, and outlines the strategic focus for the year ahead.
- **Earnings Calls:** CEOs often join analysts and investors for live Q&A sessions following quarterly results. This is where they're expected to explain key decisions, address concerns, and provide insight into the company's performance and outlook.
- **Official Filings and Reports:** While they may not draft every line, CEOs sign off on quarterly and annual reports. If there are missing details, vague disclosures, or avoided issues, it's fair to hold the CEO accountable.

To find a company's quarterly reports or earnings calls, simply look up "<company name> investor relations." All publicly traded companies should have an investor relations webpage, and this is a treasure trove of valuable information for shareholders, including links to the company's SEC filings for quarterly and annual reports.

Whether you're reading a shareholder letter or listening to an earnings call, you're ultimately trying to answer one simple question: Is this person being honest, clear, and transparent, or are they dancing around the truth? You should ask yourself some questions:

1. Do they explain complex issues clearly, or are they hiding behind jargon?
2. Are they open about challenges, or do they only focus on the positives?
3. When something goes wrong, do they take responsibility, or blame external factors?
4. Do they sound like a thoughtful leader, or more like a politician dodging hard questions?
5. After reading or listening, do I trust them more, or less?

These five questions, when thoughtfully applied, help keep your analysis grounded. When it comes to assessing management, a healthy dose of skepticism goes a long way because while numbers rarely lie (barring outright fraud), people sometimes do. Whether you're reading an annual report, tuning into an earnings call, watching a CEO interview, or reading a shareholder letter, these questions act as a filter, helping you spot when a leader is truly aligned with long-term shareholders or when they're more focused on their own reputation or compensation.

Consider the following excerpts from Warren Buffett's recent shareholder letters as an example of what genuine transparency and shareholder-first leadership looks like:

Berkshire's per-share market value *dropped* by 5.3% in 2020, while the S&P 500 gained 18.4%.

—2020 Shareholder Letter

Over the years, Berkshire has attracted an unusual number of such "lifetime" shareholders and their heirs. We cherish their presence and believe they are entitled to hear every year both the good and bad news, delivered directly from their CEO and not from an investor-relations officer or communications consultant forever serving up optimism and syrupy mush.

—2023 Shareholder Letter

During the 2019–23 period, I have used the words "mistake" or "error" 16 times in my letters to you. Many other huge companies have never used either word over that span. Amazon, I should acknowledge, made some brutally candid observations in its 2021 letter. Elsewhere, it has generally been happy talk and pictures.

—2024 Shareholder Letter

While these are just a few excerpts, they reveal a consistent theme: Buffett doesn't hide. He openly acknowledges underperformance, uses blunt language when discussing mistakes, and takes pride in delivering truth directly to shareholders. This is exactly the kind of person you want running a business: honest, transparent, and grounded.

Now let's contrast that with a very different kind of CEO—Elizabeth Holmes, founder of Theranos. While Buffett embraced transparency, Holmes built her company on secrecy, hype, and half-truths. Theranos claimed it could run hundreds of medical tests from just a few drops of blood, but when questioned, Holmes offered vague answers or invoked confidentiality. She famously told CNBC in 2015, "First they think you're crazy, then they fight you, then you change the world," doubling down on the vision instead of addressing the growing skepticism. Internally, employees were silenced with strict nondisclosure agreements and a culture of fear. Externally, investors were fed a story that wasn't backed by working technology. The result? A $9 billion valuation built on smoke and, eventually, criminal fraud charges.

Another important measure of a CEO's integrity is how transparent the company is in its reporting. In the United States (and in many other parts of the world) public companies are legally required to disclose specific information to ensure fairness and protect investors. For example, in the United States, the Securities and Exchange Commission (SEC) mandates a series of filings that must be made available to the public. (See Table 9.1.) These can typically be found on a company's investor relations website, and each document comes with detailed disclosure requirements.

While these filings offer valuable information, they can still be dense or confusing, especially for investors without a background in finance or accounting. The raw numbers alone often don't tell the full story. That's why a high-integrity CEO plays such a critical role: they

Table 9.1   SEC Filings

Form	Purpose
Form 10-K	Annual report: includes audited financials, risk factors, management's discussion and analysis, executive compensation, and more
Form 10-Q	Quarterly report: includes unaudited financials, updates on operations
Form 8-K	Used to report material events (e.g., CEO change, major lawsuit, acquisition)
Proxy Statement (DEF 14A)	Sent before shareholder meetings; includes executive pay, board info, voting matters
Form S-1	Required for companies planning an initial public offering
Form 4	Discloses insider trading activity by executives and directors

should help shareholders understand the business, not hide behind complexity.

And since they're the ones signing off on the reports, it's fair to expect that they not only understand the numbers but can explain them too.

One of the best ways to test this is by diving into the annual report. Two key sections in particular reveal a lot about a CEO's communication style and priorities:

1. **Part I, Item 1: Business Description**
2. **Part II, Item 7: Management's Discussion and Analysis**

These are the same sections we focused on in Chapter 6, and these sections give the CEO and management team a chance to explain the business in plain language. How they use that opportunity says a lot. A high-integrity CEO will aim to make these sections clear, insightful, and accessible, helping you genuinely understand what the business does, how it makes money, and how it performed over the past year.

Let's start with the business description. This part should tell you—in no uncertain terms—what the company does and how its operations generate revenue. If you're met with vague jargon, buzzwords, or corporate fluff instead of clarity, that's not a good sign.

To see this in action, take a look at Meta's 2024 Annual Report.

We report financial results for two segments: **Family of Apps (FoA)** and **Reality Labs (RL)** [emphasis added]. Currently, we generate substantially all of our revenue from selling advertising placements on our family of apps to marketers, which is reflected in FoA. Ads on our platform enable marketers to reach people across a range of marketing objectives, such as generating leads or driving awareness. Marketers purchase ads that can appear in multiple places including on Facebook, Instagram, Messenger, and third-party applications and websites. RL generates revenue from sales of consumer hardware products, software, and content. (Meta Platforms, Inc., 2024)

That sounds pretty good so far. A clear breakdown that Meta has two main business segments, and that most of the revenue comes in from ads across their family of apps. Let's read on to get more context on the two business segments.

Family of Apps Products

- **Facebook.** Facebook helps give people the power to build community and bring the world closer together. It's a place for people to share life's moments and discuss what's happening, nurture and build relationships, discover and connect to people with shared interests, and create economic opportunity. They can do this through Feed, Reels, Stories, Groups, Marketplace, and more.

- **Instagram.** Instagram brings people closer to the people and things they love. Instagram Feed, Stories, Reels, Live, and messaging are places where people and creators can connect and express themselves through photos, video, and private messaging, and discover and shop from their favorite businesses.

- **Messenger.** Messenger is a simple yet powerful messaging application for people to connect with friends, family, communities, and businesses across platforms and devices through text, audio, and video calls.

- **Threads.** Threads is an application for text-based updates and public conversations, where communities come together to discuss topics of interest. People can connect directly with their favorite creators and others who love the same things or build a loyal following of their own to share their ideas, opinions, and creativity with the world.

- **WhatsApp.** WhatsApp is a simple, reliable, and secure messaging application that is used by people and businesses around the world to communicate and transact in a private way. Within WhatsApp we launched WhatsApp Channels, a one-to-many broadcast service designed to help people follow information from people and organizations that are important to them.

Reality Labs Products

Many of our Reality Labs investments are directed toward long-term, cutting-edge research and development for products that are not on the market today and may only be fully realized in the next decade. This includes exploring new technologies such as neural interfaces using electromyography, which lets people control their devices using neuromuscular signals, as well as innovations in AI and hardware to help build next-generation interfaces. In the near term, we are continuing to develop early metaverse and wearables products and experiences that help people feel connected, anytime, anywhere.

Our metaverse efforts include our VR, MR, and social platform initiatives. Our current product offerings in VR include our Meta Quest devices, as well as software and content available through the Meta Horizon Store, which enable a range of social experiences that allow people to defy physical distance while engaging in gaming, fitness, entertainment, and more. To drive greater adoption and acceptance of VR we have introduced MR capabilities, which allow users to experience the immersion and presence of VR while still being grounded in the physical world, through our Meta Quest devices.

Our wearables efforts include our AR initiatives. We have continued to advance our roadmap to include additional AI-enabled offerings such as the RayBan Meta AI glasses, which feature Meta AI, our advanced conversational assistant, as well as other features such as hands-free interaction. As we continue our long-term efforts to bring AR glasses to market, in 2024 we also unveiled our Orion prototype, a pair of true AR glasses that overlay content on top of the physical world. It does this with an industry-leading field of view and in glasses form factor for comfortable wear.

In general, while all of these investments are part of our long-term initiative to help build the next computing platform, our metaverse efforts also include notable shorter-term projects developing specific products and services to go to market, whereas our wearables efforts are primarily directed toward longer-term research and development projects. For example, in 2025, we expect to spend approximately 50% of our Reality Labs operating expenses on our wearables initiatives, and the remaining 50% on our metaverse initiatives. We apply significant judgment in estimating this expense breakdown as there are certain shared costs across product lines, and our expectations are subject to change, including as the next computing platform and our business strategies evolve. In particular, we regularly evaluate our product roadmaps and make significant changes as our understanding of the technological challenges and market landscape and our product ideas and designs evolve. (Meta Platforms, Inc., 2024)

That's quite a bit of detail. While I did cut out some fluffy preamble, overall, I'd rate this description pretty highly. The report opens with a straightforward explanation of Meta's two business segments, Family of Apps (FoA) and Reality Labs (RL). And while it clearly states that "substantially all of our revenue comes from selling advertising placements on our family of apps," it's refreshing that Meta still includes a thorough description of their "Reality Labs" business, which is an initiative requiring significant investment (and incurring significant operating losses) at the current time.

The report also gives a functional breakdown of Meta's products, giving a clear, consumer-facing description of its major platforms (Facebook, Instagram, WhatsApp, Messenger, Threads) and what users typically do on each one. For someone unfamiliar with Meta's ecosystem, this section does a good job of explaining why these apps matter and how they support the business model.

And finally, the discussion of Reality Labs goes well beyond surface-level commentary. It describes short- and long-term projects, the distinction between metaverse and wearables efforts, and even provides a breakdown of expected spending in 2025 (50% on wearables, 50% on metaverse). This level of forward-looking guidance and breakdown of priorities suggests a strong effort at transparency.

> **The Verdict:** The spending breakdown, the acknowledgment of speculative R&D, and the segment summaries all reflect a genuine effort to keep shareholders informed. There are occasional lapses into buzzword-laden or optimistic phrasing, particularly in describing hardware initiatives, but that doesn't significantly undermine the overall quality of communication. I give them an 8/10.

Once you've read through the business description (Part I, Item 1), the next step is to carefully review Management's Discussion and Analysis (Part II, Item 7). This section gives the leadership team a chance to explain what happened over the past year, not just in numbers, but in context. It's also one of the easiest places to assess integrity.

As you read, ask yourself:

- Are they explaining *why* revenue or profits changed, or just stating that they did?
- Are they open about challenges and missed goals, or only focused on the wins?

- Do they link performance to specific strategic decisions, like new products, cost-cutting, or pricing changes?
- Do they offer a *measured* outlook on the future, or just broad, optimistic statements?

Take this excerpt from Meta's 2024 Annual Report as an example:

FoA revenue in 2024 increased $29.35 billion, or 22%, compared to 2023. The increase was almost entirely driven by advertising revenue.

Advertising revenue in 2024 increased $28.68 billion, or 22%, compared to 2023 due to increases in ad impressions delivered and average price per ad.

This is exactly what transparent communication should look like. It doesn't just present growth, it explains why that growth occurred. Meta directly links the increase in revenue to more ad impressions and higher pricing, giving investors a clear view into what's driving the business. There's no fluff, no jargon, no attempt to obscure the results, just a straightforward explanation that helps shareholders understand what's working. This kind of clarity and precision builds trust and makes it easier for long-term investors to confidently evaluate the company's direction.

Another sign of transparent leadership is the willingness to speak openly about areas of business that aren't profitable. In Meta's 2024 annual report, management doesn't shy away from acknowledging the significant drag Reality Labs has had on company performance:

Some of these investments, particularly our significant investments in Reality Labs, have generated only limited revenue and reduced our operating margin and profitability, and we expect the adverse financial impact of such investments to continue for the foreseeable future. For example, our investments in Reality Labs reduced our 2024 overall operating profit by approximately $17.73 billion, and we expect our Reality Labs investments and operating losses to increase in 2025.

This level of candor stands out. Rather than disguising Reality Labs as a booming growth engine or downplaying the cost, Meta openly quantifies the hit to profits and signals that those losses are expected to grow in the near term. That kind of forward-looking honesty is rare—and valuable. It suggests that leadership is focused on building trust with shareholders, not simply telling them what they want to hear. For investors trying to assess CEO integrity, this is exactly the kind of frank commentary that builds confidence.

In the end, how a CEO communicates (especially during difficult times) is one of the clearest indicators of their integrity. The best leaders don't just report results; they explain them. They admit to mistakes, weigh up trade-offs, and speak to shareholders with the honesty of a business partner rather than the polish of a politician. If you come away from a letter, earnings call, or annual report with a clearer understanding of the business and greater trust in the person leading it, that's a strong sign you're dealing with someone who respects their shareholders. It's a rare and valuable quality. But communication is only the first test. The next place to look for alignment (or a lack of it) is the CEO's paycheck.

Watch How CEOs Are Paid

Taking a closer look at how a CEO is paid is one of the most objective ways to assess whether they're truly aligned with shareholders. As Charlie Munger famously put it, "Show me the incentive, and I'll show you the outcome." If you want to understand a CEO's priorities, follow the money. Incentives drive behavior, and for a CEO, the way they're paid can reveal whether their interests are aligned with long-term shareholders or not. A well-designed pay package rewards long-term performance and encourages smart, sustainable decision-making. A poorly structured one can do the opposite, encouraging short-term thinking, risky bets, or even manipulation of financial data.

Executive compensation is detailed in a company's proxy statement, officially known as SEC Form DEF 14A. This document outlines how the CEO—and the broader executive team—are paid, breaking down the structure of their compensation plans. It should clearly disclose the specific performance metrics, targets, and key performance indicators (KPIs) the CEO must meet to unlock various components of their pay, along with the exact dollar amounts tied to each.

Table 9.2 shows the various ways a manager can be compensated.

None of these compensation elements are inherently bad, but what matters is how they're structured and weighted. To assess whether a CEO's incentives are aligned with long-term shareholders, we need to look at how much they earn *in each category*, and what conditions must be met for them to get paid. The question we need to answer is simple: are they being rewarded for building lasting value?

For example, imagine a founder-CEO who owns 20% of the company, takes no salary, and receives only long-term restricted stock units (RSUs) and performance stock units (PSUs) tied to multiyear shareholder returns. That's exactly what we like to see. In this case, the CEO makes money the same way we do, by growing the value of the business over time. If the stock performs well, so do they. If it doesn't, they feel it too.

Now imagine the opposite: a CEO with little or no equity ownership, a $20 million salary, and a $10 million cash bonus if earnings per share (EPS) increase by 10% next year. This is a very different picture. Not only are they being paid a fortune regardless of performance, but their big bonus depends on a single short-term metric. That creates a dangerous incentive: rather than focusing on building long-term value, this CEO might pursue short-term financial engineering to hit their EPS target.

One common tactic is share buybacks. When a company buys back its own shares, it reduces the total number of shares outstanding. That means even if total earnings stay flat, the earnings per share rises, on paper. If the stock is undervalued, buybacks can be a smart

Table 9.2   Executive Compensation Categories

Category	What It Is	Why It Matters
Base Salary	Fixed annual cash payment	Provides stability but usually makes up a small portion of total compensation
Cash Bonus	Short-term incentive, usually tied to annual performance goals	Can motivate short-term results, but may encourage short-term thinking
Stock Options	The right to buy company shares at a fixed price (usually lower than market)	Rewards stock price growth, but can lead to risky behavior if misaligned
Restricted Stock Units (RSUs)	Company shares granted to the manager over time, often with vesting requirements	Encourages retention and alignment with shareholder value
Performance Stock Units (PSUs)	Shares awarded only if specific long-term targets are met	Focuses attention on long-term strategic goals
Deferred Compensation	Portion of pay set aside to be received later, often for tax or retention reasons	May show long-term commitment, but can hide total compensation from view
Perks and Benefits	Noncash extras (e.g., car allowance, private travel, insurance, club fees)	Often minor in value but can raise red flags if excessive
Pension/ Retirement Plans	Post-career benefits or contributions to retirement savings accounts	Can be generous, especially in legacy companies
Stock Ownership (Personal Investment)	Shares the CEO has purchased or holds personally (not granted by the company)	Strong sign of alignment and represents "skin in the game"

capital allocation move. But if the stock is overvalued, buybacks destroy shareholder value in the long run. Still, for a CEO chasing a short-term EPS boost, the incentive to pull this lever is strong, regardless of whether it's in the shareholders' best interest.

Let's take a look at one of the most controversial compensation packages in corporate history: the performance award granted to Tesla and SpaceX CEO, Elon Musk. His 2018 Tesla pay deal made headlines around the world and has been the subject of multiple legal challenges, most notably being struck down *twice* by a Delaware judge. But while the $56 billion figure attached to the package sounds outrageous, the real question is: Was it actually bad for Tesla shareholders?

Rather than receiving a salary or any sort of cash bonus, Musk's deal was entirely performance based. He was granted a series of 12 tranches of stock options, each tied to ambitious operational and market capitalization goals. (See Table 9.3.) Stock options give the holder the right to buy the company's shares at a fixed price (called a *strike price*) regardless of what the stock is trading at later. In Musk's case, after adjusting for Tesla's two stock splits, the strike price was set at $23.33 per share, which reflected Tesla's market value at the time the package was signed in early 2018.

Here's where it gets interesting: for every $50 billion increase in Tesla's market cap, Musk unlocked another tranche of options at that same $23.33 strike price. So, as the company became more valuable, Musk's ability to buy discounted shares became exponentially more lucrative. The higher the stock climbed, the more money he stood to make. That kind of structure strongly aligns his financial success with that of long-term shareholders. If the goal is to add hundreds of billions of dollars in market value, then Musk is directly incentivized to make that happen.

But market cap alone wasn't enough. To vest each tranche, Tesla also had to meet specific revenue or EBITDA targets, adding an important layer of accountability. This ensured that Tesla wasn't just inflating its valuation with hype; the business had to *actually perform*. By tying Musk's reward to both top-line growth and bottom-line execution, the board designed a package that rewards results, not just stock market speculation. And boy, did Elon Musk follow through? Today, Tesla's market cap sits at more than $1 trillion, a staggering

Table 9.3   Elon Musk's 2018 Compensation Package

Tranche	Market Cap Milestone	Options Granted to Musk	Strike Price	Market Price (Est.)	Musk's Profit per Option (Est.)	Value of Tranche to Musk at Time of Vesting (Est.)
1	$100B	25,330,050	$23.33	$31.05	$7.72	$195,547,986
2	$150B	25,330,050	$23.33	$46.57	$23.24	$588,670,362
3	$200B	25,330,050	$23.33	$62.09	$38.76	$981,792,738
4	$250B	25,330,050	$23.33	$77.62	$54.29	$1,375,168,415
5	$300B	25,330,050	$23.33	$93.14	$69.81	$1,768,290,791
6	$350B	25,330,050	$23.33	$108.66	$85.33	$2,161,413,167
7	$400B	25,330,050	$23.33	$124.19	$100.86	$2,554,788,843
8	$450B	25,330,050	$23.33	$139.71	$116.38	$2,947,911,219
9	$500B	25,330,050	$23.33	$155.23	$131.90	$3,341,033,595
10	$550B	25,330,050	$23.33	$170.76	$147.43	$3,734,409,272
11	$600B	25,330,050	$23.33	$186.28	$162.95	$4,127,531,648
12	$650B	25,330,050	$23.33	$201.80	$178.47	$4,520,654,024

rise from when the deal was signed. By the time a Delaware judge moved to invalidate the agreement (a whole other story), the pay package had grown to be worth more than $56 billion to Musk.

But beyond his stock option package, there's another major reason Elon Musk is aligned with long-term shareholders: his enormous personal stake in the company. This is one of the most powerful ways to evaluate whether a CEO's interests are truly aligned with yours. As of early 2025, Musk owns approximately 715 million Tesla shares, representing around 20.5% of the company's outstanding stock. At current market prices, that stake is worth more than $300 billion.

In simple terms, no one benefits more from Tesla's long-term success than Elon Musk himself. The company's future share price is the single biggest driver of his net worth. This is the ultimate example of "skin in the game." With so much personal wealth tied to Tesla's stock, Musk is financially motivated to make decisions that enhance long-term shareholder value. His interests aren't just aligned with yours; they're welded to them.

Apple CEO Tim Cook is another high-profile executive making millions of dollars per year, but his compensation package looks much different to Musk's. Table 9.4 shows a summary of his different compensation categories, taken from Apple's 2025 Proxy Statement.

That's a lot to take in, but it's worth slowing down and reading the proxy filing carefully to see exactly how each reward was determined. In the next section, we'll walk through each category in turn and then step back to make a judgment call once we've seen the full picture.

Base Salary

Tim Cook earns a base salary of $3 million per year. This is the fixed amount he gets just for doing the job, no matter how Apple performs. That number hasn't changed since 2016.

Cash Bonus

On top of his salary, Cook is eligible for a cash bonus of up to $6 million each year. The size of the bonus depends on how well Apple performs against two targets:

- Revenue
- Operating Income

For 2024, Apple's board set "threshold," "target," and "maximum" goals for each. The bonus payout depends on which levels are met:

- If only the minimum (threshold) is hit, Cook gets 50% of his salary ($1.5 million).
- If target level is hit, Cook gets 100% of his salary ($3 million).
- If maximum is hit, Cook gets 200% of his salary ($6 million).

Table 9.4 Tim Cook's 2024 Compensation

Category	What It Is	Details (2024)	Why It Matters
Base Salary	Fixed annual cash payment	$3 million; unchanged from prior years	Stable and modest relative to total comp; avoids overpaying for simply showing up
Cash Bonus	Short-term incentive based on revenue and operating income targets	$6 million, the maximum possible based on Apple's results	Puts focus on growth of two numbers that are difficult to manipulate
Time-based RSUs	Stock awards that vest over time regardless of performance	$12.5 million, vesting in three tranches across 4.5 years	Encourages retention and rewards tenure; still linked to stock value
Performance Stock Units (PSUs)	Stock units that vest only if performance goals are hit	$37.5 million, with the amount realized dependent on Apple's total shareholder return vs other S&P 500 companies	Strongly aligns with shareholder outcomes; encourages outperformance
Other Compensation	401(k) plan, healthcare programs, product discounts, employee stock purchase plans, etc.	Special perks for Cook include security detail, private jet usage, but includes no golden parachute clauses	Can occasionally be a way to give excessive additional perks to a CEO, not related to performance
Stock Ownership	Personal investment in company shares	Cook owns $651 million worth of Apple shares	Gives Cook skin in the game; aligns with long-term shareholders

Source: Adapted from Apple Inc., (2025)

Figure 9.1   Tim cook's cash bonus calculation.

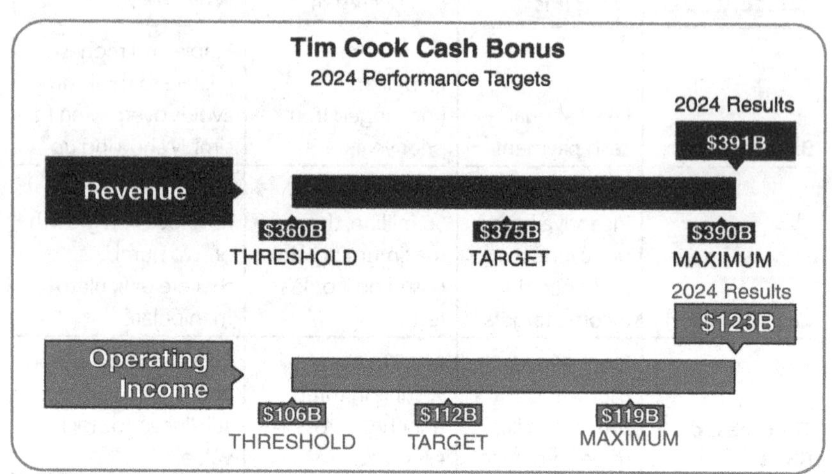

As shown in Figure 9.1, in 2024, Apple exceeded the maximum targets for both revenue and operating income, so Cook received the full $6 million bonus.

Stock Awards (RSUs)

The biggest part of Cook's pay package is made up of stock awards, specifically the following:

- Performance-based RSUs—75%
- Time-based RSUs—25%

Let's break each down.

Time-based RSUs

These are Apple shares Cook receives over time, just for staying in the role. In 2024, Apple awarded him time-based RSUs worth $12.5 million, based on Apple's stock price at the time of the grant. These shares don't vest all at once: he'll receive one-third every 1.5 years, starting April 1, 2026. This encourages Cook to stick around.

Table 9.5   Allocation of Tim Cook's Performance-based RSU

Apple's TSR vs S&P 500 Peers	Percentage of Target RSUs Cook Gets
Top 85% or higher	200% (double)
55th Percentile	100% (target)
25th Percentile	25%
Below 25%	0% (none)

Performance-based RSUs

These shares are only awarded if Apple performs well compared to other S&P 500 companies. Specifically, Apple looks at total shareholder return (TSR) over a three-year period. The better Apple performs, the more shares Cook receives, as you can see in Table 9.5.

For 2024, Cook was granted performance RSUs worth $37.5 million, and the exact number of shares he gets will depend on how Apple performs from 2024 to 2026.

Previous Performance Example

In October 2023, Cook vested in performance RSUs that had been granted back in 2020. Because Apple ranked in the 70.77th percentile of the S&P 500 over that three-year period, Cook received 511,000 RSUs, about 153% of the original target. See Table 9.6.

Other Compensation

Beyond salary and stock, Tim Cook receives a few extra benefits, most of which are standard at Apple. He's eligible for the company's 401(k) plan, healthcare, product discounts, and an employee stock purchase plan. He can also defer part of his salary or bonus into a long-term savings plan, which is common for executives.

Given his high-profile role, Apple also requires Cook to fly private for all travel and provides personal security. While these

Table 9.6   Apple's Performance vs S&P 500 Companies

	Relative TSR Percentile	TSR Results for Three-year Performance Period
Apple	70.77th Percentile	54.09%
	85th Percentile	87.50%
	55th Percentile	30.60%
S&P 500 Companies	25th Percentile	−0.17%
	Below 25th	<−0.17%

are expensive services, they're considered necessary business expenses, not personal perks. Cook pays tax on personal travel and receives no reimbursement. He may also attend Apple-sponsored events, and if they're considered taxable benefits, he covers the tax himself.

Stock Ownership

And now for the cherry on top, Tim Cook's personal ownership of Apple stock, or what investors often call "skin in the game." According to Apple's 2025 Proxy Statement, Cook owns 3,280,180 shares of Apple, valued at approximately $651 million at the time of writing. For context, *Forbes* estimates his net worth at around $2.4 billion, meaning more than a quarter of his wealth is currently tied to Apple's stock price.

This level of ownership far outweighs any single bonus or equity grant. For example, that complex performance-based RSU award we broke down earlier, valued at $37.5 million, is just 5% of what he already holds in Apple stock. In other words, it's not a stock award or bonus that drives his financial future; it's Apple's long-term performance. And that's exactly what shareholders want: a CEO whose success depends on building value for everyone.

SO, WHAT'S THE CONCLUSION?

Based on the structure and incentives within Tim Cook's compensation package, it's clear that Apple has taken a thoughtful and shareholder-aligned approach. Cook's fixed salary remains modest by CEO standards and hasn't increased since 2016, which signals restraint and avoids rewarding tenure alone. His bonus is tied to measurable financial outcomes (revenue and operating income), which are core drivers of Apple's value. While some might argue that $6 million is a generous payout, it only comes when the company hits its most ambitious targets, as it did in 2024.

Where Cook's alignment with long-term shareholders really shines is in the stock component of his compensation. The majority (75%) of his equity awards are performance-based and hinge on Apple outperforming other companies in the S&P 500 over a three-year period (a difficult feat due to Apple's massive scale). This incentive structure has worked exceptionally well since Cook became CEO back in 2011. From that date through the end of 2024 Apple's cumulative TSR increased approximately 1,908%, significantly outpacing the S&P 500, and Apple's market capitalization grew by more than $3 trillion. This incentive structure discourages short-term decision-making and rewards sustained performance. Even the time-based RSUs, which vest gradually, serve to keep Cook focused on the company's long-term future.

Add to this his significant personal stake in the business—owning more than $650 million in Apple stock—and you have a CEO whose financial success is overwhelmingly tied to the long-term performance of the company. That level of "skin in the game" is rare, and it reinforces that Cook is incentivized to think like an owner, not just an employee.

The Verdict: Tim Cook's compensation package is a strong example of shareholder alignment. It balances smaller near-term company performance metrics with longer-term incentives and is backed by meaningful personal ownership from Cook himself. Almost every part of it rewards Cook for doing the same thing investors want: growing Apple's value over time. I give it 8.5/10.

While Tim Cook's pay structure is a strong example of shareholder alignment, unfortunately, not all CEOs are incentivized with the same discipline or transparency. In fact, some executive compensation packages have done serious damage, not only to a company's value, but to shareholder trust. One of the most infamous examples of this comes from the early 2000s, involving Tyco International and its former CEO, Dennis Kozlowski.

Tyco was once a sprawling industrial conglomerate with operations spanning electronics, healthcare, security systems, and fire protection. Under Kozlowski's leadership, the company grew rapidly through a wave of acquisitions, and for a time, it was a Wall Street darling (even featuring in the S&P 500). But behind the scenes, Kozlowski's personal compensation package was raising eyebrows. Unlike Tim Cook's structure, which is heavily weighted toward long-term performance and shareholder return, Kozlowski's pay relied on aggressive bonuses, vague performance goals, and unchecked access to company resources. And if that wasn't shocking enough, Kozlowski was also awarded *unauthorized* loans from the company, which did nothing but fund his lavish lifestyle, including artwork, luxury real estate, and a $2 million birthday party in Sardinia, complete with an ice sculpture of Michelangelo's *David* dispensing vodka.

From a shareholder's perspective, the problem wasn't just the extravagance; it was that Kozlowski had no real financial reason to think long term. His incentives were built around short-term earnings manipulation, not sustainable value creation. He wasn't building ownership or waiting for performance-based stock to vest over years. Instead, he was maximizing his personal benefit regardless of the company's trajectory or the risks it was taking. There was no "skin in the game," and ultimately, Tyco's stock collapsed under the weight of scandal. The company's stock price plummeted from a high of nearly $60 in December 2001 to around $18 by December 2002, erasing billions in shareholder value (Auburn University, n.d.). Investor confidence was shattered, leading to a significant loss in market capitalization and a tarnished corporate reputation.

In 2005, Dennis Kozlowski was convicted of fraud, conspiracy, and grand larceny. He served more than six years in prison. Tyco's reputation was badly damaged, and shareholders paid the price. It remains a textbook example of how poorly designed compensation and a lack of board oversight can devastate a company's long-term value.

This contrast with Apple's current leadership couldn't be clearer. Where Cook's wealth is tied to Apple's long-term performance and shareholder outcomes, Kozlowski's pay was untethered from results and fueled by short-term excess. For investors, this story is a powerful reminder: how a CEO is paid matters deeply, not just for the executive's behavior, but for the health and future of the business itself.

When evaluating a business, the quality of the management team is one of the most important (and often underestimated) factors. It's simple: a great CEO can amplify the strengths of a business with a moat, while a poor one can erode even the most powerful competitive advantage. That's why Warren Buffett and other long-term investors spend so much time assessing leadership, not just the numbers.

Remember, when it comes to integrity, two of the most revealing areas are how a CEO communicates and how they're compensated. If a CEO speaks plainly, owns their mistakes, and keeps shareholders informed through both good times and bad, that's a strong signal.

Pair that with a compensation package tied to long-term performance (and ideally, significant personal stock ownership) and you can be confident they're acting like an owner, not just an employee.

That said, assessing management isn't an exact science. There's no formula for integrity, and modern compensation structures can be notoriously complex. This is where your judgment as an investor comes in. Ask the right questions, apply a healthy dose of skepticism, and trust your instincts. If something feels off, or if the CEO's incentives don't align with yours as a long-term shareholder, it may be best to keep looking.

CHAPTER TEN

ASSESSING MANAGEMENT'S TALENT

While integrity is essential when evaluating a CEO, it's only half the story. A leader can be honest and well-meaning, but if they consistently make poor decisions, shareholders still lose. As Charlie Munger once quipped, his favorite type of business is *"one that can stand a little mismanagement but doesn't get it."* This chapter is about making sure your company doesn't get it either.

When we talk about whether management is doing a good job, we're really talking about their ability to allocate capital wisely. In other words, we're examining how they choose to use the company's money, and just as importantly, where they get it from. Are they piling on debt unnecessarily? Are they buying back shares at inflated prices? Are they wisely using the retained earnings to reinvest in the business? These decisions speak volumes about a leader's financial judgment and long-term thinking.

So, how do we assess whether a CEO truly has *talent,* not just integrity? We focus on three key areas:

1. **Return on invested capital:** Are they generating strong returns on the money they reinvest?
2. **Dividends and buybacks:** Are they returning capital to shareholders in intelligent, value-enhancing ways?
3. **Debt management:** Are they using leverage responsibly or recklessly putting the company at risk?

RETURN ON INVESTED CAPITAL

Getting déjà vu? That's understandable. Return on invested capital (ROIC) is one of those rare metrics that pulls double duty. It's a great way to assess whether a business has a moat, yes, but it's also one of the most powerful indicators of management's decision-making ability.

Remember, ROIC tells us how effectively a company is reinvesting its money to generate profits. In other words, when the business earns a dollar and puts it back to work (whether by expanding operations, developing new products, or acquiring another company), ROIC tells us what return those reinvestments are generating. And since it's the management team making those capital allocation decisions, ROIC becomes a direct reflection of their judgment and skill.

A high and consistent ROIC (15% or more) means leadership isn't just growing the business; they're doing so efficiently and intelligently, allocating capital into high-return opportunities rather than chasing growth for growth's sake. It's one thing to expand; it's another to expand *profitably.* Crucially, ROIC filters out the illusion of growth.

A company might be growing revenue or even earnings, but if it's constantly pouring more money into the business just to maintain that growth (without strong returns), then shareholder value isn't really increasing. Worse, it might be shrinking.

Ultimately, great managers think like investors: they want the highest return for each dollar put to work. The ROIC helps us measure whether they're achieving that. And if they're not? It could be a sign of poor capital allocation, a weakening moat, or both.

Now, since we've already covered ROIC in Chapter 8 (see the "Capital Efficiency Test"), I'll keep this explanation brief. And here's an added bonus: the test we're going to use to assess a CEO's talent is the exact same "Capital Efficiency Test" we already used. That's because ROIC not only tells us how efficient the business is, it also tells us how smart the decision-makers are.

Alright, alright … let's go through it again for those at the back.

The Capital Efficiency Test has three parts. First, we calculate the company's current ROIC. As a rule of thumb, investors like Warren Buffett tend to favor businesses with an ROIC above 15%, while anything under 10% is usually a deal breaker. That tells us how profitable the company's most recent reinvestments have been.

Second, we look at ROIC over the past 10 years for a more thorough assessment. Then finally, we examine how that ROIC is *trending* over time. Is it stable? Is it improving? Or is it slowly declining?

This trend is where we get a clear window into the talent and discipline of the management team. If ROIC is improving over time, it means the management team is finding increasingly profitable opportunities to reinvest in, a clear sign of a capable CEO who's allocating capital wisely. That's exactly what we want to see.

On the flip side, if ROIC is declining year after year, it suggests that the business is getting lower returns from each dollar it reinvests. Maybe the industry is maturing, or maybe the CEO is simply running out of good ideas. Either way, a falling ROIC tells us that capital

Table 10.1   Alphabet ROIC (Past 10 Years)

Year	ROIC (%)
2015	13
2016	13
2017	9
2018	16
2019	15
2020	15
2021	25
2022	23
2023	25
2024	28

is being deployed with decreasing effectiveness. And as long-term investors, that's a red flag we can't ignore.

So, with that in mind, let's revisit two examples from earlier, starting with Alphabet (Google). Table 10.1 shows how its ROIC has trended over time.

While some year-to-year fluctuations are to be expected, the long-term trend is what matters, and it's hard to ignore. Google's ROIC has climbed steadily from 13% in 2015 to an impressive 28% in 2024. That kind of growth tells us two important things.

First, it reinforces what we've already discussed about Google's competitive advantage. Sustained and rising ROIC is often a hallmark of a business with a strong moat, one that allows it to reinvest profits into high-return opportunities year after year.

But second (and just as importantly), this rising ROIC speaks volumes about the skill of the management team, particularly CEO Sundar Pichai. Over nearly a decade, Alphabet hasn't just maintained its dominance; it's become more efficient, more focused, and more profitable in how it reinvests capital. That doesn't happen by accident.

Quite simply, an ROIC of 28% suggests that Pichai and his leadership team are not only making smart strategic bets but that their capital allocation decisions are *getting better over time.* Far from losing his edge, Pichai seems to be sharpening it. And for long-term shareholders, that's a very encouraging sign. It's one thing to inherit a great business; it's another to keep improving it.

Consider, on the other hand, General Motors. Table 10.2 shows the table of its ROIC since 2016.

A 10% ROIC in the most recent year (2024) isn't terrible, and it's certainly not the lowest you'll come across. But when we zoom out and look at the bigger picture, the story becomes clearer: this management team hasn't moved the needle. Over the past six years, ROIC has barely budged. It's flat. Stable, yes, but also stagnant.

And while some might argue there's value in consistency, what we're really seeing is a business and a leadership team that appears to be stuck in its ways. There's no upward trend, no evidence of smarter capital allocation, and no signal that management is unlocking new, more profitable opportunities. At best, investors can expect more of the same: a steady, unremarkable 10% return on reinvested capital.

Table 10.2   General Motors ROIC (Past 10 Years)

Year	ROIC (%)
2016	15
2017	0.6
2018	11
2019	10
2020	10
2021	11
2022	11
2023	11
2024	10

To be clear, 10% ROIC isn't a disaster. But it's also not something that gets long-term, Buffett-style investors excited, especially when you consider what's possible under great leadership. The contrast between a company like General Motors, posting a flat 10%, and a company like Google, steadily lifting its ROIC from 13% to 28% over the past decade, couldn't be starker.

One business is treading water. The other is compounding value. I know which management team I'd want steering my capital.

DIVIDENDS AND BUYBACKS

Dividends and share buybacks can reveal a lot about whether management is truly focused on creating long-term value for shareholders or just chasing short-term performance targets. But before we dive into the details, let's quickly define each of these terms.

Dividends are straightforward. They're payments a company makes to its shareholders simply for owning the stock. Technically, they represent a distribution of profits, but you can think of it as a per-share cash reward. For example, in 2024, Coca-Cola paid out a massive $8.4 billion in dividends, which worked out to $1.94 per share.

Share buybacks are another way companies return profits to shareholders. In this case, the company uses its own cash to buy back its shares on the open market, just like you or I might. But here's the key difference: when a company buys back its shares, those shares are typically deleted, reducing the total number of shares outstanding. The size of the pie hasn't changed, but now there are fewer slices, meaning each remaining slice is worth more. For long-term shareholders, this means their ownership stake in the company has quietly increased. They didn't buy more shares, but thanks to the buyback, their existing shares now represent a larger piece of the business. In essence, it's a subtle and tax-efficient way to increase shareholder value, but only when done wisely.

And that's the key phrase here: *"when done wisely."* For both dividends and share buybacks, *timing and context matter.* Sometimes they're exactly the right move. Other times, they're a complete waste of shareholder capital. Let's start with dividends.

As we've discussed, dividends are a simple way for companies to return profits to shareholders. They give you cold hard cash in your bank account simply for holding the stock. That sounds great in theory. But as long-term investors, we need to think deeper.

Let's go back to ROIC. Imagine a company with a world-class CEO who's generating a 40% ROIC, meaning for every $1 reinvested into the business, they're earning $0.40 in profit. That's incredible. So, if the company can consistently reinvest profits at a 40% return, should the CEO be paying those profits out as dividends?

Absolutely not.

Why? Because if management can invest money that effectively, the best thing they can do for their shareholders is keep reinvesting. Paying out a dividend would force you, the investor, to go and find somewhere else to put that money, and earning anything close to a 40% return isn't exactly easy.

This is why many long-term, Buffett-style investors prefer low or no dividends from great businesses. Take Berkshire Hathaway, for example. It's famously never paid a dividend. Alphabet, under Sundar Pichai, consistently earns a strong ROIC (currently around 28%) and only pays a token dividend—just 0.57%—because management believes the money can be used more effectively inside the business than outside it.

The takeaway is this: don't rule out a company just because it doesn't pay a dividend. Sure, some investors (like retirees) need income from their portfolio. But if you're younger and focused on long-term growth, you're often better off investing in businesses where great management is putting your money to work at high rates of return.

But with that said, what if the company in question has only a low ROIC? To be honest, we probably wouldn't be looking at a business in this ballpark, but if this were the case, the logic flips. If management can't find good reinvestment opportunities (if every dollar they reinvest is only generating mediocre returns), you'd much rather they just hand the profits back to you. Why? Because you can likely put that money to better use elsewhere. In these cases, paying a dividend (or even buying back shares) is the honest and shareholder-friendly thing to do. What you don't want is management clinging to capital and reinvesting it in low-return or failed projects just for the sake of growth. That's a fast track to destroying shareholder value.

A share buyback is another tool to return profits to shareholders, but the *timing* of these repurchases is what really highlights the skill of the management team. Think about it this way: as investors, we aim to buy shares when they're undervalued (when the stock price is trading below our estimate of the business's intrinsic value). We'll explore how to calculate that intrinsic value in more detail in later chapters, but for now, all we need to understand is the basic idea that, as investors, we're trying to buy low.

The exact same principle applies to companies repurchasing their own shares. Management should be acting like value investors, using company funds to buy back shares only when they're trading at a discount to intrinsic value. That's how buybacks create value for long-term shareholders. But if, for example, Apple's stock is trading at twice its intrinsic value, and Tim Cook decides to spend billions of company profits buying back shares at that inflated price, that's not smart capital allocation. That's no different than an individual investor knowingly overpaying for a stock. Instead of creating value, the company is destroying it.

Unfortunately, this kind of poor timing was on full display in the US airline industry during the late 2010s. American Airlines, Delta,

United, and Southwest operate in a notoriously tough business: capital intensive, cyclical, and ultra-competitive. So, when a rare stretch of strong profitability hit in the decade following the global financial crisis, management had some big decisions to make.

Let me ask you this: what would *you* do with a surge in profits if you ran one of these enormous companies? Pay down debt? Build a cash buffer for the inevitable downturn? Upgrade the fleet or expand routes? Any of those would be sensible, long-term decisions.

But instead of building financial resilience, US airlines chose to return the bulk of their profits to shareholders through aggressive share buybacks, often at elevated prices as their stocks soared to all-time highs. According to a 2020 Bloomberg report, the four major carriers (American, Delta, United, and Southwest) spent a staggering 96% of their free cash flow from 2010 to 2019 on buybacks (Kochkodin, 2020). So, when COVID-19 brought global travel to a standstill, the industry was dangerously unprepared.

It's a textbook case of poor capital allocation: during the good times, management focused on boosting short-term shareholder returns rather than strengthening the balance sheet for inevitable downturns. And when that downturn arrived, shareholders narrowly avoided a catastrophic wipeout, not because of brilliant leadership, but because the US government stepped in with more than $50 billion in emergency support through loans and payroll grants.

The bailouts sparked a huge wave of public criticism. Taxpayers were now footing the bill to rescue companies that had spent the previous decade prioritizing financial engineering over long-term stability. In response, the government attached strict conditions to the aid, including a ban on buybacks and dividends for a set period, ensuring that public funds weren't used to enrich executives or shareholders during the crisis.

On the other hand, a well-executed share buyback can add tremendous value to shareholders. Warren Buffett and his management of Berkshire Hathaway is a perfect example. Buffett has long said he will only repurchase shares when they are trading below intrinsic value, ensuring that every buyback increases the ownership stake and long-term value for remaining shareholders. He's patient, disciplined, and treats shareholder capital as if it were his own.

A great example came in 2020, during the COVID-19 market panic. While many companies were slashing buybacks to preserve cash, Buffett did the opposite. He recognized that Berkshire's stock was trading well below what he believed it was worth, and he moved decisively, spending a record $24.7 billion on share repurchases that year alone. That was more than five times the amount from 2019 (Seeking Alpha, 2025).

Rather than overpaying for growth or appeasing short-term investors, Buffett used the market's fear as an opportunity to quietly boost shareholder ownership at a discount. No fanfare, no market timing, just classic value investing applied at the company level. For long-term shareholders, it was a masterclass in how to use buybacks to build lasting wealth.

So, what's the summary?

Both dividends and buybacks are powerful tools, but only when used wisely. The key is *context*. With that said, here are some simple rules you can come back to when evaluating the CEO of a company on your personal watchlist.

1. **Reinvest when ROIC is high.**
   If the company can consistently reinvest profits at a high return (e.g., 15%+), that's where the capital should go. Dividends can wait.
2. **Return capital when reinvestment opportunities are weak.**
   If ROIC is low and profitable opportunities are limited, management should return cash to shareholders through dividends or buybacks.

3. **Only buy back shares when they're undervalued.**

   A buyback only adds value if the stock is trading below intrinsic value. Otherwise, it's just financial engineering that destroys shareholder wealth.

4. **Treat shareholder capital like your own.**

   Great CEOs think like owners. They should always allocate capital carefully, patiently, and with long-term compounding in mind.

DEBT MANAGEMENT

By looking at ROIC, dividends, and share repurchases, we've been assessing *how* a company allocates the capital it has. But there's another equally important question: *where* does that capital come from? Is the business funding growth through its own profits? Is it raising money from investors? Or is it borrowing, taking on debt to finance its ambitions?

How a company uses debt is a direct reflection of the judgment of its CEO and leadership team. When used wisely, debt can amplify success, turning a good business into a great one. But when overused or mismanaged, it can become a major liability, sometimes even bringing the company down.

The real danger arises when a company takes on more debt than it can comfortably repay. In good times, this might not seem like a problem. But when the tide goes out (when profits drop or the economy slows), those debt obligations don't go away. And that's when poor debt management can turn into a crisis.

To understand just how damaging debt can be, let's take a closer look at cruise industry giant Royal Caribbean (RCL). Like many capital-intensive businesses, Royal Caribbean requires massive upfront investment—building billion-dollar ships, maintaining a global presence, and spending heavily on marketing to fill cabins. On its own, this isn't necessarily a problem. Some industries (like cruising, airlines, utilities, and telecoms) naturally require substantial infrastructure spending. The danger comes when companies take on more debt than they can realistically manage, especially without a contingency plan for rough seas ahead.

In Royal Caribbean's case, the company had taken on significant long-term debt to fuel its fleet expansion, operating under the assumption that tourism demand would remain steady. But when COVID-19 brought global travel to a standstill in early 2020, revenue collapsed virtually overnight, yet the debt obligations remained. With roughly $8.4 billion in long-term debt and annual interest payments exceeding $400 million, Royal Caribbean suddenly found itself in a financial fight for survival (Royal Caribbean Cruises Ltd., 2020).

The debt load meant the company had no cushion. With interest payments looming and no income to cover them, the stock price plummeted from around $130 to a low of $19.09 on March 18, 2020. But the pain didn't stop there. To avoid default, Royal Caribbean was forced to raise capital by issuing new shares, a move that deeply diluted existing shareholders. Unlike a share buyback, which reduces the number of shares and increases each shareholder's stake, a capital raise does the opposite: it slices the pie into more pieces, making every share worth less.

During 2020, the company raised approximately $9.3 billion of new capital through a combination of bond issuances, capital raises, and other loan facilities. When it came to stock issuances, the company had no choice but to flood the market with tens of millions of new shares, dramatically expanding the share count. Investors who had already watched the value of their holdings plunge were now seeing their ownership diluted as well. It was a double blow: first from the share price collapse and second from dilution. And while issuing new equity may have been necessary to keep the business alive, it stands as a powerful reminder of what happens when companies take on too much debt in good times and are forced to pay the price in the bad.

To avoid getting caught in situations like Royal Caribbean, Buffett-style investors focus on two key financial checks: leverage and liquidity. First, we want to make sure the company hasn't taken on excessive debt. Once that box is ticked, the next step is to assess whether the company has enough cash and short-term assets to cover its obligations. In other words, even if it has some debt, can it pay the bills when they come due? Fortunately, there are two simple ratios that help us answer these questions: the debt-to-equity ratio (to measure leverage) and the current ratio (to assess liquidity).

The Debt-to-equity Ratio

The debt-to-equity ratio tells us how a company is financing its operations, specifically, how much of its capital structure is funded by debt versus equity. In simple terms, it shows whether the business is leaning more on borrowed money or its own (and its shareholders') resources.

The formula is straightforward:

$$\text{Debt-to-equity Ratio} = \frac{\text{Total Debt}}{\text{Shareholders' Equity}}$$

Both "total debt" and "shareholders' equity" are easy to find on a company's *balance sheet*. Shareholders' equity typically appears near the bottom of the balance sheet, representing the company's net assets after liabilities are subtracted. Total debt is the sum of short-term borrowings (found under current liabilities) and long-term debt (found under noncurrent liabilities). By adding those two together and dividing by the shareholders' equity, you get a quick snapshot of how much the company relies on debt relative to its own capital base.

A high debt-to-equity ratio means the company is heavily reliant on borrowing, which can magnify both gains and losses. This might be acceptable in stable, cash-generating businesses like utilities, but in cyclical or unpredictable industries, it's a red flag. Buffett has always preferred companies with low debt and strong returns on equity, those that don't need to rely on borrowed money to grow.

As a general rule, a debt-to-equity ratio below 1 is considered conservative, while anything much above 2 can be a sign that the company is leaning too heavily on borrowed money. Now, it's true that context matters—what's considered high for a software company might be perfectly normal for a capital-intensive telecom firm—but for our purposes, aiming for businesses with a ratio under 1 is a solid benchmark. And when you find a company with a debt-to-equity ratio below 0.5, that's a strong signal you're looking at a management team that values financial resilience over financial engineering, exactly the kind of mindset long-term investors want to partner with.

Take a look at Table 10.3 to see how some of the world's largest companies compare.

Table 10.3   Debt-to-equity Ratios of US-listed Companies

Company	Total Debt (US$B)	Total Equity (US$B)	Debt-to-equity Ratio
Alphabet (Google)	$28.50	$345.27	0.08
Nvidia	$10.29	$83.84	0.12
Meta Platforms	$49.52	$185.03	0.27
Microsoft	$105.02	$321.89	0.33
Apple	$98.19	$66.80	1.47
General Motors	$134.16	$66.43	2.02
Royal Caribbean	$20.12	$8.14	2.47

As you can see from the data, debt-to-equity ratios vary widely across companies and tell us a lot about management's approach to financial risk. Tech giants like Alphabet, Nvidia, and Meta all maintain extremely conservative capital structures, with debt-to-equity ratios well below 0.3, reflecting a strong preference for financial flexibility and resilience. Even Microsoft, despite carrying more than $100 billion in debt, keeps its ratio low thanks to an enormous equity base. Contrast that with companies like General Motors and Royal Caribbean, where debt levels exceed equity by more than 2-to-1. These higher ratios reflect greater financial risk and reduced flexibility, especially in times of crisis. For long-term, Buffett-style investors, these numbers serve as a clear reminder: the lower the leverage, the more likely the business can survive and thrive through uncertain times.

The Current Ratio

While the debt-to-equity ratio tells us how much a company relies on debt, the current ratio gives us a snapshot of its short-term financial health, specifically, whether it has enough resources on hand to meet its obligations over the next 12 months.

The formula is simple:

$$\text{Current Ratio} = \frac{\text{Current Assets}}{\text{Current Liabilities}}$$

Both figures are easy to locate on a company's balance sheet. Current assets typically appear at the top of the asset section and include lines like cash, marketable securities, accounts receivable, and inventory, essentially anything the company expects to convert into cash within a year. Current liabilities are listed under the liabilities section and include short-term debts, accounts payable, accrued expenses, and other obligations due within 12 months. By dividing the current assets by current liabilities, you get a quick and clear picture of whether the company has the liquidity to cover its immediate financial responsibilities.

As a general rule, a current ratio of 1 or higher suggests the company has enough short-term assets to cover its short-term liabilities. A ratio above 2 is often seen as a healthy margin of safety. But if the ratio falls below 1, it's a big warning sign that the company might not be able to meet its near-term obligations without borrowing or selling off assets.

Again, this is another metric where industry context matters. A fast-moving retailer or tech platform with steady cash flow and rapid inventory turnover might function perfectly well with a current ratio just above 1. These businesses can quickly convert inventory to cash and don't need a large cushion. In contrast, capital-intensive companies like manufacturers or airlines (where revenues can be unpredictable and expenses are high) should ideally maintain a higher current ratio to protect against unexpected disruptions.

My personal rule of thumb is to look for a current ratio above 1.5. Even when industry norms might justify lower ratios, I prefer a wider margin of safety. When it comes to liquidity, I'd rather steer clear of businesses that are even flirting with financial tightropes.

Table 10.4 shows the same table of companies we examined before, but now showing their current ratios instead.

As Table 10.4 shows, there's a wide range of liquidity profiles across major public companies. Nvidia stands out with a remarkably strong current ratio of 3.39, followed by Meta at 2.66, both suggesting ample short-term financial flexibility. Alphabet also maintains a healthy cushion at 1.77, comfortably above the 1.5 benchmark. Microsoft, while slightly lower at 1.37, still maintains a solid liquidity position, likely aided by consistent operating cash flow from its subscription model. On the other end of the spectrum, Apple's

Table 10.4   Current Ratios of US-listed Companies

Company	Current Assets (US$B)	Current Liabilities (US$B)	Current Ratio
Alphabet (Google)	$162.05	$91.65	**1.77**
Nvidia	$89.94	$26.54	**3.39**
Meta Platforms	$90.23	$33.89	**2.66**
Microsoft	$156.64	$114.21	**1.37**
Apple	$118.67	$144.57	**0.82**
General Motors	$110.01	$90.75	**1.21**
Royal Caribbean	$1.83	$10.30	**0.18**

current ratio of 0.82 may raise eyebrows, but this is more a reflection of its efficient working capital management and steady cash flow than any immediate risk. General Motors, at 1.21, sits just above the minimum safety threshold of 1, while Royal Caribbean is the clear outlier, with a dangerously low current ratio of 0.18. That figure signals serious liquidity risk, reinforcing everything we've discussed: when a crisis hits, companies with thin margins for error can find themselves in deep trouble fast. For investors focused on long-term stability, a strong current ratio is one of the clearest indicators that a company is equipped to survive whatever comes next.

RECOGNIZING WHAT MAKES A GOOD CEO

In the end, assessing the talent of a CEO isn't just about charisma or communication; it's about how they think. And nothing reveals how a leader thinks more clearly than how they source and allocate capital. We've looked at how management reinvests earnings (ROIC), how and when they return excess cash to shareholders (dividends and buybacks), and how they handle financial risk (debt and liquidity). These are the levers that CEOs can directly control, and over time, their choices in these areas separate the truly exceptional managers from the rest.

A great CEO doesn't just grow a business; they grow it intelligently. They avoid the traps of overpaying for growth, overleveraging the balance sheet, or playing to the crowd with flashy buybacks at the wrong time. Instead, they focus on long-term compounding, disciplined capital deployment, and protecting the downside. They think like investors because they are investors. They treat shareholder capital like their own.

As investors, our job is to recognize that talent. The tools we've covered in this chapter (ROIC, capital return policy, debt-to-equity, and current ratio) help us go beyond the surface. They allow us to separate lucky leaders riding tailwinds from those who are truly skillful stewards of capital. So, take a moment to look under the hood. Study the trends. Ask the hard questions. Because when we partner with a talented, rational, and shareholder-aligned CEO, we're not just investing in a stock. We're compounding alongside someone who knows how to turn every dollar into two. And that's how real wealth is built for long-term shareholders.

CHAPTER ELEVEN

VALUATION

The first three pillars of the Buffett/Munger investment approach (understanding the business, checking for a moat, and analyzing management) are all about identifying a wonderful business. These three tick boxes tell us whether we've found a great company. But it's Buffett's final pillar, valuation, that takes the next step of determining whether our "wonderful business" could potentially become a "wonderful investment."

Remember Charlie Munger's famous one-minute breakdown of the strategy? He put it simply:

> No matter how wonderful it is, it's not worth an infinite price, so we have to have a price that makes sense and gives a margin of safety, considering the natural vicissitudes of life.

And that's exactly what we need to do. Once we've identified a great company, we need to estimate its intrinsic value so that we can determine if the current share price makes sense. As Buffett often reminds us, not all wonderful companies are necessarily wonderful investments. So how do we calculate the true value of a company's shares? Well, that's exactly what we'll dive into in this chapter.

The easiest way to get yourself in the right headspace to understand business valuation is to think of all companies simply as money-making machines. Imagine you're at a garage sale and you stumble upon a rusty machine that prints money. That's all it does. Now, putting aside any legal concerns for a moment, you check out the machine, flip the switch, it starts whirring, and a few seconds later it spits out a $10 bill. Amazing! A machine that literally prints money. Of course, you decide you must buy it.

But then the owner tells you it's going to cost you $2,000. Seems steep for such a rusty old contraption, right? But hey, it prints money. So, how much should you offer?

At this point, there are a few key questions you need to be able to answer to determine the right price:

1. How much cash can it print per day?
2. How much will it cost to maintain this machine each year, to ensure it doesn't break down?

The owner informs you that the machine can print $50 a day (in $10 bills) and should be able to keep doing this for the next 10 years, as long as it's properly maintained. However, there's a catch: maintenance costs $15,000 per year.

Naturally, you grab your calculator and start doing the math:

$$\text{Annual Cash Flow} = 365 \text{ days} \times \$50 = \$18{,}250$$
$$\text{Annual Maintenance} = \$15{,}000$$
$$\text{Annual Profit} = \$18{,}250 - \$15{,}000 = \$3{,}250$$
$$\text{Profit Over 10 Years} = \$3{,}250 \times 10 = \$32{,}500$$

The owner is asking $2,000 for the machine. After just one year, you'd make $3,250 in profit. This sounds like a great deal; after all, you'll make back your investment in less than 12 months. You decide to buy the machine.

But what if the asking price were $20,000 instead? It would take more than six years to recoup your initial investment. Is that still worth it? Probably. I'm sure we could tough it out for six years, and then we'd start seeing a profit. That still sounds like a favorable deal to me. But what if the price was $200,000? Now, it would take you 61 years to make back your investment. At that point, it might not seem like such a good deal anymore, especially since inflation could erode the value of those $10 bills over such a long period. Who knows if $10 bills will even exist in 60 years?

Now, while this example may be a bit outlandish, it highlights a key concept of valuation. Businesses are essentially money-making (or sometimes money-consuming) machines. To understand whether a company's market price is overvalued or undervalued, we need to understand the cash flow it's generating today, estimate how much it will generate in the future (while we hold the investment), and then calculate what we should pay today to ensure we're achieving a reasonable return over time.

In value investing, the key method for calculating a company's intrinsic value is the discounted cash flow analysis (DCF). The concept is simple: as investors, we imagine buying the entire company today, owning it for 10 years, collecting the cash flow it generates during that time, and then finally, selling the business on to another investor once those 10 years are up. The question we must answer is: how much should we pay for the business today to achieve our desired return over the next decade?

Let's break it down with a simple example: a lemonade stand. The kids down the street are looking to sell their business, and you're considering buying. The stand generates $1,000 in free cash flow each year and has been growing at 10% annually in recent years. The business currently holds $2,000 in cash, which it uses to replenish supplies, but it also carries $5,000 in debt that was taken on to get the business off the ground. After doing some research, you discover that over the past 10 years, lemonade stands in the area have consistently sold for a price roughly 20 times their annual free cash flow. However, the kids are unsure about the price they'd be willing to sell the business at, so how do you figure out what to offer to make sure you're getting a great deal?

There are six steps to calculating the intrinsic value of a business:

1. Projecting the future cash flows
2. Estimating the terminal value
3. Determining the price we should pay today
4. Adding the discounted cash flows
5. Adjusting for cash and debt
6. Applying a margin of safety

Let's now take the time to go through each step, to calculate the intrinsic value (the price we'd like to pay) for the lemonade stand.

STEP 1: PROJECT FUTURE CASH FLOWS

The first thing we need to do is estimate how much the business will make in free cash flow over the next 10 years. We start by taking the current free cash flow of $1,000 and growing it at the expected 10% annual growth rate. Table 11.1 shows how the numbers look.

Looking at Table 11.1, we see that over 10 years, the lemonade stand's annual cash flow will grow from $1,000 to nearly $2,600 per year if the business can maintain its 10% annual growth rate.

STEP 2: ESTIMATE THE TERMINAL VALUE

While, in reality, we hope to own our investments for many decades, for the discounted cash flow analysis, we assume that after owning the lemonade stand for 10 years, we're going to sell the business on

Table 11.1   Estimated Future Cash Flow

Years of Ownership	Estimated Free Cash Flows
0 (right now)	$1,000.00
1	$1,100.00
2	$1,210.00
3	$1,331.00
4	$1,464.10
5	$1,610.51
6	$1,771.56
7	$1,948.72
8	$2,143.59
9	$2,357.95
10	$2,593.74

to another buyer. But how do we estimate what we could sell it for? Well, over the past decade, lemonade stands in the area have typically sold for around 20 times their annual free cash flow. If this trend holds true, we can estimate the *terminal value* of the business after 10 years by multiplying the 10th year's free cash flow by 20. This gives us:

$$\text{Terminal Value} = 20 \times \$2,593.74$$
$$= \$51,874.80$$

"Terminal value" is just finance jargon for what we expect to sell the business for at the end of our 10 years of ownership. With that in mind, Table 11.2 shows the total cash flow we can expect as the owner of the lemonade stand.

Overall, we've estimated that the business will generate approximately $69,406 in cash over the next 10 years. This total includes $17,531.17 from the free cash flow we'll receive over the 10 years, plus the $51,874.80 we expect to get from selling the business at the end of

Table 11.2   Total of All Estimated Future Cash Flows

Years of Ownership	Future Cash Flow
1	$1,100.00
2	$1,210.00
3	$1,331.00
4	$1,464.10
5	$1,610.51
6	$1,771.56
7	$1,948.72
8	$2,143.59
9	$2,357.95
10	$2,593.74
Terminal Value (sale price after 10 years of ownership)	$51,874.80

year 10. Therefore, the price we pay for this business today *must* be less than that total to ensure we make a positive return. But how much less?

STEP 3: DETERMINE THE PRICE WE SHOULD PAY TODAY

To calculate the price we should pay for the lemonade stand today, we need to figure out what each future cash flow (including the terminal value) is worth in today's dollars. Why? Because money received in the future is worth less to us than money we receive today. This concept is known as the *time value of money*.

Imagine you're offered $100 today or $100 in a years' time. Mathematically, you should always choose the $100 today because you could invest it and earn a return over the next 12 months. For example, if you know you can generate a 15% annual return by investing the cash, you'd need to be promised more than $115 in 12 months to make it worth waiting for the cash.

In our case, we're targeting exactly that: a *15% annual return*. Anything less, and you might as well just invest in a passive index fund. Anything more, and you'd be aiming to be the next Warren Buffett. A 15% return strikes a reasonable balance. It's achievable over the long term without being completely out of reach.

With this goal in mind, we now need to discount all of the future cash flows by 15% annually to figure out what we should pay for each today. If we work backward, taking off our 15% return each year for every expected future cash flow, we'll end up calculating what we could pay today for those cash flows that will lock in our desired 15% return on investment. Let's use our eighth year of ownership as an example. We've estimated that in year 8, the business will generate $2,143.59 in cash flow (see Table 11.2). But here's the catch: we won't receive that cash until eight years from now. So, we need to figure out what we should pay today to make $2,143.59 represent a 15% annual return after eight years.

The formula to calculate the present value of the future cash flow is:

$$PV = \frac{FV}{(1 + r)^n}$$

where

PV = Present value (what we can pay for that cash flow today)

FV = Future value (the amount of cash we expect to receive in the future, e.g., $2,143.59 for year 8)

r = Discount rate (the desired annual return, e.g., 15% or 0.15)

n = Number of years between now and when you'll receive the cash flow, e.g., eight years

Because we expect to receive \$2,143.59 in year 8, and our desired annual return is 15%, the formula to find the present value of that future cash flow would look like this:

$$PV = \frac{2{,}143.59}{(1 + 0.15)^8}$$
$$= \frac{2{,}143.59}{3.059}$$
$$= \$700.74$$

So, the present value of \$2,143.59 (received in eight years' time) is \$700.74 (assuming a 15% annual return). In other words, if we invested \$700.74 today and earned a 15% return every year for eight years, we would end up with \$2,143.59.

But, unfortunately, that's not all: we now need to do this calculation for *every* future cash flow we expect to receive. Yes, we need to discount the cash flow we expect in the first year, the second, the third, and so on, all the way through to the 10th year. And we'll also discount the terminal value to determine what that future sale price is worth to us today. Table 11.3 has these numbers pre-filled.

As you can see, even though the business's cash flows are growing at a steady 10% each year, the price we're willing to pay for those future cash flows actually decreases. For instance, while the year 10 cash flow (\$2,593.74) is higher than the year 9 cash flow (\$2,357.95), we're willing to pay less for the year 10 cash flow today. This happens because the 15% return we're targeting as our minimum acceptable return is higher than the 10% growth rate of the business's cash flows.

We also discount the terminal value for the same reason we discount other future cash flows: money in the future is worth less than money today due to the time value of money. The terminal value represents the expected sale price of the business at the end of the investment period, but because it's realized many years down

Table 11.3 Discounting All Future Cash Flows

Year	Future Cash Flow	Discounted Cash Flow	Formula Used
1	$1,100.00	$956.52	$PV = \dfrac{1100}{(1 + 0.15)^1}$
2	$1,210.00	$914.93	$PV = \dfrac{1210}{(1 + 0.15)^2}$
3	$1,331.00	$875.15	$PV = \dfrac{1331}{(1 + 0.15)^3}$
4	$1,464.10	$837.10	$PV = \dfrac{1464.1}{(1 + 0.15)^4}$
5	$1,610.51	$800.71	$PV = \dfrac{1610.51}{(1 + 0.15)^5}$
6	$1,771.56	$765.89	$PV = \dfrac{1771.56}{(1 + 0.15)^6}$
7	$1,948.72	$732.59	$PV = \dfrac{1948.72}{(1 + 0.15)^7}$
8	$2,143.59	$700.74	$PV = \dfrac{2143.59}{(1 + 0.15)^8}$
9	$2,357.95	$670.28	$PV = \dfrac{2357.95}{(1 + 0.15)^9}$
10	$2,593.74	$641.13	$PV = \dfrac{2593.74}{(1 + 0.15)^{10}}$
Terminal Value	$51,874.80	$12,822.66	$PV = \dfrac{51874.80}{(1 + 0.15)^{10}}$

the track, we need to adjust it to reflect its present value. By discounting the terminal value, we ensure it accurately reflects what we could pay today for that future cash flow, based on our 15% required annual return. In this instance, if we're aiming to sell the business in 10 years for $51,874.80, the present value of that future cash flow is only $12,822.66, since $12,822.66 compounds to $51,874.80 at a 15% annual return over 10 years.

STEP 4: ADD THE DISCOUNTED CASH FLOWS

Now that we've discounted each future cash flow back to its present value, the next step is simple: we add up all the *discounted* cash flows to calculate an approximate intrinsic value of the business.

The intrinsic value is essentially the total amount we should be willing to pay for the lemonade stand today, based on the future cash flows it will generate. In other words, it's the sum of the present value of every future dollar we expect to receive from the business.

To calculate the rough intrinsic value, we simply add up the discounted cash flows from year 1 to year 10, plus the discounted terminal value.

Here's the formula for the intrinsic value:

$$\text{Intrinsic Value} = \Sigma\text{Discounted Cash Flows of Year 1 Through 10} + \text{Discounted Terminal Value}$$

Once we add those numbers together, we get the approximate intrinsic value, which represents the price we should be willing to pay today for the business to achieve our desired annual return of 15%.

Table 11.4 shows the sum of the discounted cash flows, including the terminal value, and thus, the rough intrinsic value of the lemonade stand.

Table 11.4   Sum of Discounted Cash Flows

Description	Amount
Total Discounted Cash Flows (Years 1–10)	$7,895.06
Discounted Terminal Value	$12,822.66
Sum of Discounted Cash Flows	**$20,717.72**

STEP 5: ADJUST FOR CASH AND DEBT

We're now very close to finalizing the intrinsic value of the lemonade stand. There's just one last adjustment to make: we need to factor in the company's cash on hand and any debts it needs to repay.

In our intrinsic value calculation, spare cash increases the price we're willing to pay (since it's an asset the business can use or distribute), while debt decreases the value (because it represents future obligations that must be paid).

Let's consider an analogy. Imagine you're looking to buy a house, and based on your research, you believe it's worth $600,000. Then, the neighbor tells you there's $100,000 buried in the backyard. What's the new price you'd be willing to pay for the house? Clearly, you'd be willing to pay $700,000 knowing the house comes with an unexpected treasure. This is similar to how businesses operate. Companies often hold cash or short-term investments for emergencies or growth, and that cash should be considered when determining the business's value.

On the flip side, let's say you inherit the house, but there's a $200,000 mortgage attached to it. The value of the house is no longer $600,000; to you it's effectively worth $400,000, since the debt must be repaid. The same logic applies to businesses. Debt represents a liability that reduces the company's overall value, as that money must be paid back before the business can distribute profits to its owners.

That said, to arrive at the final intrinsic value, we need to do the following:

1. **Add cash and cash equivalents:** Cash increases the intrinsic value of the business because it's available for reinvestment or distribution to shareholders.

Table 11.5 Intrinsic Value of the Lemonade Stand

Description	Amount
Sum of Discounted Cash Flows	$20,717.72
Cash and Cash Equivalents	+$2,000
Total Debt	−$5,000
Intrinsic Value	**$17,717.72**

2. **Subtract total debt:** Debt decreases our intrinsic value because it represents future obligations the business must fulfill, which reduces its overall worth.

In our lemonade stand example, the company has

- **$2,000 in cash** to help with the day-to-day operations and
- **$5,000 in outstanding debt** that was taken on to get the business started.

To adjust the intrinsic value, we simply add the cash and subtract the debt, as shown in Table 11.5.

And that's it! After factoring in both cash and debt, the final intrinsic value of the lemonade stand is $17,717.72. So, what does this mean? This is the amount you would be willing to pay today for the lemonade stand in order to achieve a 15% annual return on your investment over the next 10 years.

Or is it?

STEP 6: MARGIN OF SAFETY

Okay, I admit—that was mean. Just when you thought you were home, I throw in one more step. But trust me, this one is important, and it's where Buffett-style investors set themselves up to make big returns.

While we've dotted the i's and crossed the t's, and after considering all factors, we've arrived at an intrinsic value of $17,717.72 for the lemonade stand; there's one more crucial factor to account for: the unpredictability of the future.

The reality is, while the lemonade stand has been growing at 10% annually, it could face some rough years. It might only grow at 5% in the near future, or even less. The government could introduce a sugar tax, cutting into those sweet cash flows. While this example is fictional, it highlights a key truth: unexpected events happen. Take 2019, for instance. Who could have predicted that a global pandemic would disrupt the economy, leaving nearly 15% of Americans unemployed within a year?

Following Buffett's principles, we aim to protect against downside risk. After all, Rule 1 is "Don't lose money," and Rule 2 is "Never forget Rule 1." To do that, we need to expect the unexpected and build some flexibility into our intrinsic value calculation to account for the inevitable errors that come from predicting the future. This is where the margin of safety comes in, as Charlie Munger put it, to account for "the natural vicissitudes of life."

So, what do we do? Simple. We take our calculated intrinsic value and shave a bit off the top. How much? Personally, I look for a minimum margin of safety of 30%, but many Buffett-style investors aim for 50%. Why? Two reasons. First, it protects you from downside risk if things don't go as planned. But second, if you *can* buy a business at half its intrinsic value, your upside is enormous. It not only protects your capital but supercharges your potential returns. Let's go back to the lemonade stand in Table 11.6.

We estimated that under normal conditions, buying the business for $17,717.72 would likely deliver a 15% annual return over 10 years. But if we manage to buy it for just $8,858.86, not only do we dramatically increase the likelihood of still hitting that 15% return even if things go wrong, but if the business performs as expected and

Table 11.6   Lemonade Stand Margin of Safety

	Amount ($)
Intrinsic Value	$17,717.72
30% Margin of Safety	$12,402.40
50% Margin of Safety	$8,858.86

the external environment remains smooth, our annual return could end up far exceeding 15%. This is how investors like Warren Buffett, Mohnish Pabrai, Peter Lynch, Li Lu, and Bill Ackman generate out-sized returns. They wait patiently for those rare moments when the market offers a high-quality business at a steep discount, then they swing hard.

That's the beauty of the margin of safety. It gives you room to be wrong and still come out right. It shifts the odds in your favor, turning uncertainty into opportunity. You're no longer relying on perfect predictions or flawless execution; instead, you're building in a buffer that protects your downside and enhances your upside. In a world full of unknowns, the margin of safety is your most powerful tool. It's what separates speculation from smart investing, and it's what gives you the confidence to act when opportunity finally knocks.

So how would we approach the negotiation for the lemonade stand? We'd likely start with an aggressive offer, our 50% margin of safety price, around $8,850. Ideally, the kids accept, and we lock in an incredible deal. But if not, we might be willing to negotiate up to our maximum price of $12,400, which still gives us a comfortable 30% margin of safety. Beyond that? We walk. If they're asking $16,000, we politely decline. Because at that point, we're no longer investing with a margin of safety; we're hoping the next 10 years go perfectly. And that's not how value investors operate. We don't leave our returns up to chance. Instead, we add the lemonade stand to our watchlist, stay patient, and wait for the next great opportunity.

CHAPTER TWELVE

WARREN BUFFETT'S BEST INVESTMENT

Now that we've walked through the valuation process using a fictional example, let's look at how this method plays out in the real world, specifically, with one of the greatest investments Warren Buffett has ever made: Apple.

Buffett began buying Apple stock in 2016. At the time, this move surprised many investors. Apple was seen as a tech company, a sector Buffett had famously avoided for years. But what Buffett saw in Apple wasn't just a technology business. He saw an incredibly strong brand, a sticky ecosystem, a loyal customer base, and a cash machine hiding in plain sight. In his view, Apple wasn't a traditional tech stock; it was a consumer products company with deep competitive advantages and a predictable stream of earnings and cash flow.

Between 2016 and early 2020, Berkshire Hathaway invested around $35 billion into Apple. Fast forward to December 2023, and

Apple had become Berkshire's largest single holding, making up around 30% of the entire stock portfolio.

At its peak, Berkshire's Apple stake was worth just over $180 billion, a more than 5× return on the original investment in just seven years. That's the power of buying a high-quality business at a reasonable price, holding patiently, and letting compounding do its thing.

Of course, Buffett didn't arrive at this decision by accident. He and his team applied the same valuation logic we've just explored, estimating Apple's future earnings and cash flows, determining what those were worth in today's dollars, and only buying when the stock traded well below its intrinsic value. Let's explore the investment opportunity of Apple when Berkshire first started investing, back at the start of 2016.

STEP 1: PROJECT FUTURE CASH FLOWS

As of Apple's 2015 annual report (released in October 2015), the company's free cash flow over the previous 12 months was $70.019 billion. Free cash flow is reasonably straightforward to calculate from the *cash flow statement*: simply subtract capital expenditures (listed as "payments for acquisition of property, plant, and equipment") from "cash generated by operating activities."

For Apple in 2015, the equation looked like this:

Free Cash Flow = Cash from Operating Activities −
             Purchase of Property, Plant, and Equipment
        = $81,266,000,000 − $11,247,000,000
        = $70,019,000,000

This is always our starting point in a discounted cash flow (DCF) analysis. The next step is to estimate how fast the business might grow over the next 10 years and apply that growth rate annually to project future cash flows.

In our lemonade stand example, we assumed a simple 10% growth rate based on recent performance. But how do we estimate a growth rate for a real company like Apple? The approach I use is to look at the historical trends: I list the last 10 years of net income, shareholder equity, and free cash flow, and examine how each has grown over time.

For Apple, that looks like Table 12.1. (And just a quick heads-up—since we're now dealing with numbers in the billions and trillions, this chapter's tables will report most figures in *millions*.)

Now, that's just a whole bunch of numbers in a table, which isn't all that helpful on its own. What we really want to understand is how each financial metric has grown over the short, medium, and long term. So, using a compound annual growth rate (CAGR) calculator I found on Google, I put together the information in Table 12.2 to break it down more clearly.

From Table 12.2, it looks like Apple was growing at an impressive rate (between 30% and 40%) across the 10 years leading up to Buffett's investment. But one number should immediately catch your eye: equity. While net income and free cash flow were growing strongly, equity was barely moving. In fact, it grew just 7% in the most recent year. That's a yellow flag. I wouldn't feel comfortable applying a high growth rate like 30% annually without understanding why one of the key financial lines is lagging so far behind.

In Apple's case, a quick look at the cash flow statement clears things up: share buybacks. In 2015 alone, Apple spent $35.25 billion repurchasing its own shares, following $45 billion the year before, and $22.86 billion in the 12 months to September 2013.

When a company buys back its own shares, it reduces the number of shares available in the market, but it also reduces shareholders' equity. That might sound odd at first. Isn't the company just shifting money around? Not quite. When a business uses cash to repurchase shares, it lowers its assets (cash), and at the same time, those repurchased shares

Table 12.1 Historical Growth of Apple's Net Income, Equity, and Free Cash Flow

Financial Indicator	Sep-05	Sep-06	Sep-07	Sep-08	Sep-09	Sep-10	Sep-11	Sep-12	Sep-13	Sep-14	Sep-15
Net Income ($M)	1,328	1,989	3,495	6,119	8,235	14,013	25,922	41,733	37,037	39,510	53,394
Equity ($M)	7,428	9,984	14,531	22,297	31,640	47,791	76,615	118,210	123,549	111,547	119,355
Free Cash Flow ($M)	2,275	1,563	4,735	8,505	9,015	16,590	33,269	42,561	45,501	50,142	70,019

Table 12.2   Growth Rate of Net Income, Equity, and Free Cash Flow

Financial Indicator	10-year CAGR	5-year CAGR	1-year CAGR
Net Income	44.69%	30.67%	35.14%
Equity	32.01%	20.09%	7.00%
Free Cash Flow	40.87%	33.37%	39.64%

are held as treasury stock, which is recorded as a negative entry in the equity section of the balance sheet. So, equity drops.

For example, if a company has $1 billion in equity and uses $100 million in cash to buy back shares, its equity drops to $900 million. The business itself isn't necessarily worth less, but from an accounting standpoint, its equity has shrunk. This is why buybacks often lead to an increase in return on equity (ROE), not because profits are growing, but because the denominator (equity) is smaller. It's a subtle accounting dynamic, but a crucial one for investors to understand.

The short version? We can safely exclude equity from our growth rate estimate for Apple. Once we understand that the shrinking equity is simply a result of share buybacks (not declining business performance), the picture becomes clearer. Across the 10 years leading up to Buffett's investment, Apple was growing at an impressive 30–40% per year. But what growth rate should we assume going forward?

That's a tough question because 30–40% is extremely high, particularly for a company as large as Apple. It's much harder to grow a $500 billion company (Apple's approximate market cap in 2016) than a $5 billion one, no matter how strong its moat. In 2005, Apple generated just $2.28 billion in free cash flow. A decade later, that number had exploded to $70 billion, a 30× increase. But is it realistic to think they could repeat that and reach $2.1 trillion in free cash flow over the next 10 years? Probably not.

This is where it's crucial that we've taken the time to properly understand the business. Ultimately, the growth rate you choose to put on a business is a judgment call, and the more you understand the company and its long-term runway, the more confident you will be in assuming an annual growth rate on its future. In Apple's case, while recent history suggests a 30–40% annual growth rate would be appropriate, I'm going to take a more conservative route and use a 20% annual growth rate. It's still strong, and it reflects Apple's incredible brand and durable competitive advantages. But it's also grounded in the reality that massive growth gets harder as companies scale. At the end of the day, estimating growth comes down to both the numbers and your understanding of the business. And in this case, 30% just doesn't pass the sniff test.

So, with that said, if we apply a 20% growth rate to Apple's free cash flow over the next 10 years, where do we end up? Let's fill out Table 12.3 and find out.

Looking at Table 12.3, we see that over 10 years, Apple's annual cash flow is expected to grow from $70.02 billion to around $433.54 billion per year if the business can maintain a 20% annual growth rate.

Table 12.3   Apple's Estimated Future Cash Flows

Years of Ownership	Estimated Free Cash Flows ($M)
0 (right now)	$70,019
1	$84,023
2	$100,827
3	$120,993
4	$145,191
5	$174,230
6	$209,076
7	$250,891
8	$301,069
9	$361,283
10	$433,539

STEP 2: ESTIMATE THE TERMINAL VALUE

The next step is to estimate what we could sell Apple for after 10 years of ownership. In the lemonade stand example, we simply assumed a terminal value of 20 times free cash flow based on what similar businesses were selling for. But with a publicly traded company like Apple, we can be more precise. We can actually look back at its historical price-to-free-cash-flow (P/FCF) multiples.

To do this, you've got a few options. The first is to take the company's market capitalization on the day each annual report was released and divide it by that year's free cash flow (which you calculate by subtracting *capital expenditures* from *cash from operations* on the cash flow statement). Alternatively, you can compare the share price to the free cash flow per share. And if you want a quick shortcut, head over to a website called MacroTrends—they track historical price-to-free-cash-flow ratios for many companies. It's a bit of a cheeky hack, but one I use all the time. What we want to look at is the price-to-free-cash-flow multiple for the past five years, and from that you'll get a reliable sense of what multiple the market has typically assigned to the business. This gives you a much more grounded estimate for your terminal value. Table 12.4 shows this for Apple for the five years leading up to Warren Buffett's investment.

The average? 9.82. Let's run with that. We're going to assume that in 10 years from now we're going to be able to sell the business for at least 9.82 times the estimated free cash flow:

Table 12.4   Apple's Historical Price to Free Cash Flow Multiple

	2011	2012	2013	2014	2015
P/FCF	9.03	12.52	8.45	10.88	8.21

Table 12.5   Apple Future Cash Flows and Terminal Value

Years of Ownership	Future Cash Flow ($M)
1	$84,023
2	$100,827
3	$120,993
4	$145,191
5	$174,230
6	$209,076
7	$250,891
8	$301,069
9	$361,283
10	$433,539
Terminal Value (after 10 years of ownership)	$4,257,353

$$\text{Terminal Value} = 9.82 \times \$433,539,000,000$$
$$= \$4.257 \text{ trillion}$$

With that in mind, let's update our table to reflect all future cash flows we could expect, if we were the owner of Apple, as shown in Table 12.5.

STEP 3: DETERMINE THE PRICE WE SHOULD PAY TODAY

To calculate the price we should pay for Apple today, we now need to figure out what each future cash flow (including the terminal value) is worth in today's dollars. Remember the time value of money? We now need to discount each year's cash flow to ensure that whatever money we put down now, we're going to get a minimum of 15% returns on it each year. See Table 12.6.

Table 12.6   Apple's Discounted Future Cash Flows

Years of Ownership	Future Cash Flow ($M)	Discounted Cash Flows ($M)	Formula Used
1	$84,023	$73,063	$PV = \dfrac{84{,}023}{(1 + 0.15)^1}$
2	$100,827	$76,240	$PV = \dfrac{100{,}827}{(1 + 0.15)^2}$
3	$120,993	$79,555	$PV = \dfrac{120{,}993}{(1 + 0.15)^3}$
4	$145,191	$83,014	$PV = \dfrac{145{,}191}{(1 + 0.15)^4}$
5	$174,230	$86,623	$PV = \dfrac{174{,}230}{(1 + 0.15)^5}$
6	$209,076	$90,389	$PV = \dfrac{209{,}076}{(1 + 0.15)^6}$
7	$250,891	$94,319	$PV = \dfrac{250{,}891}{(1 + 0.15)^7}$
8	$301,069	$98,420	$PV = \dfrac{301{,}069}{(1 + 0.15)^8}$
9	$361,283	$102,699	$PV = \dfrac{361{,}283}{(1 + 0.15)^9}$
10	$433,539	$107,164	$PV = \dfrac{433{,}539}{(1 + 0.15)^{10}}$
Terminal Value (after 10 years of ownership)	$4,257,353	$1,052,353	$PV = \dfrac{4{,}257{,}353}{(1 + 0.15)^{10}}$

STEP 4: ADD THE DISCOUNTED CASH FLOWS

Now that we've discounted each of Apple's future cash flows back to their present value—as of early 2016, when Berkshire first began buying—the next step is to add them all together. This gives us an estimate of the company's intrinsic value at that time.

As a quick reminder, here's the formula we're using to calculate intrinsic value, which for Apple results in Table 12.7:

$$\text{Intrinsic Value} = \Sigma\text{Discounted Cash Flows of Year 1 Through 10} + \text{Discounted Terminal Value}$$

Table 12.7   Total Discounted Cash Flows for Apple

Description	Amount ($M)
Total Discounted Cash Flow (Years 1–10)	$891,486
Discounted Terminal Value	$1,052,353
Sum of Discounted Cash Flows	**$1,943,839**

STEP 5: ADJUST FOR CASH AND DEBT

As with our lemonade stand example, the second last step in the process is to adjust the intrinsic value. Why? To account for both the cash hoard and the debt owed by the business. Remember, we need to do the following:

1. **Add cash and cash equivalents:** Cash increases the intrinsic value of the business because it's available for reinvestment or distribution to shareholders.
2. **Subtract total debt:** Debt decreases our intrinsic value because it represents future obligations the business must fulfill, which reduces its overall worth.

In Apple's 2015 annual report, the business reported the following relevant line items (found on the *balance sheet*):

Cash and Cash Equivalents

- Cash and cash equivalents = $21,120 million
- Short-term marketable securities (treasury bonds) = $20,481 million

Total Debt

- Commercial paper (short-term unsecured corporate debt) = $8,499 million
- Current portion of long-term debt = $2,500 million
- Long-term debt = $53,463 million

(Apple Inc., 2015)

Putting it all together, we get Table 12.8.

Table 12.8   Adjusting the Intrinsic Value

Description	Amount ($M)
Sum of Discounted Cash Flows	$1,943,839
Cash and Cash Equivalents	+$41,601
Total Debt	−$64,462
Intrinsic Value	**$1,920,978**

We made it. After applying our discounted cash flow analysis to Apple as of January 2016, I would've estimated its intrinsic value at around $1.92 trillion. But remember, we don't stop there. Imagine Charlie Munger's ghost sitting on your shoulder, whispering: "Remember the natural vicissitudes of life!"

STEP 6: MARGIN OF SAFETY

Now that we've estimated Apple's intrinsic value (based on the information available in early 2016), it's time to apply our margin of safety. Why? Because no matter how careful or conservative we've been, forecasting the future is still an inexact science. The margin of safety gives us that crucial buffer to protect against errors, surprises, or misjudgments. So, let's go ahead and apply both our minimum 30% margin of safety, and our gold standard, 50%.

Looking at Table 12.9, we can see that if Apple's market capitalization was less than $1.34 trillion in January 2016, we'd be interested, and if there's any chance the market cap was less than $960 billion, we'd be getting really excited.

Well, in January 2016, Apple's market cap was a mere **$534 billion.**

Table 12.9   Applying Margin of Safety to Apple

Description	Amount ($M)
Intrinsic Value	$1,943,839
30% Margin of Safety	$1,344,685
50% Margin of Safety	$960,489

THE RESULT

In 2016, Apple's shares were trading at a *steep* discount to their intrinsic value, and Buffett didn't hesitate. He backed up the truck. Over the following few years, Berkshire went on a buying spree, accumulating more than a billion Apple shares. It was one of those rare moments where the market served up a pitch right in Buffett's sweet spot, and he swung with conviction. See Table 12.10.

Buffett invested approximately $35 billion into Apple over just a few years, after investors had turned bearish on the company. Apple had reported its first-ever decline in iPhone sales (driven more by market saturation than any real business flaw), but Wall Street feared the worst. On top of that, concerns about Apple's heavy dependence on China (both as a manufacturing hub and as a key consumer market), combined with a general cooling toward tech stocks in early 2016, led Mr. Market to severely undervalue the company. For a brief window, this wide-moat, cash-gushing giant was trading at a price-to-earnings ratio of just 11.

Table 12.10 Berkshire Hathaway's Apple Position

13F Period	Action	Shares Held
Q1 2016	Buy	39,246,988
Q2 2016	Add 55.20%	60,910,808
Q4 2016	Add 276.68%	229,438,608
Q1 2017	Add 125.52%	517,428,424
Q2 2017	Add 0.65%	520,767,840
Q3 2017	Add 3.00%	536,371,128
Q4 2017	Add 23.30%	661,335,848
Q1 2018	Add 44.90%	958,270,532
Q2 2018	Add 5.17%	1,007,823,508
Q3 2018	Add 0.21%	1,009,915,116

Figure 12.1   Apple's share price since 2016.

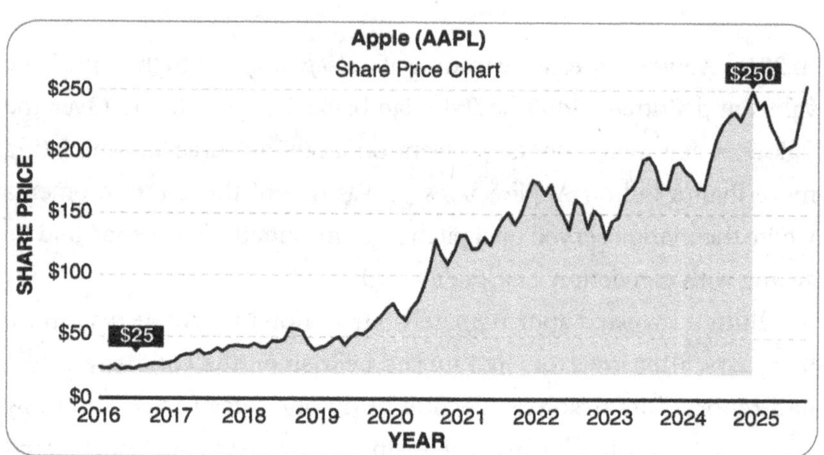

What happened next? Sure enough, as the short-term fears faded, the business kept compounding cash flow as it had for the previous decade, and the stock price surged. Over the following years, Apple's share price soared from $25 to over $250, where it sits today. (See Figure 12.1.) Buffett's Apple position ballooned in size, eventually making up more than 50% of Berkshire's US stock portfolio. The investment performed so well that even Buffett, who famously "holds forever," began trimming the position. From Q4 2023 to Q3 2024, Berkshire locked in profits on more than 615 million shares, roughly 60% of its original stake. To this day, Apple remains Berkshire's single most successful investment by dollar amount, and in 2025, Apple shares still take up about 25% of Berkshire's US portfolio.

But before we move on, there's something important to reflect on: how accurate was our discounted cash flow analysis? Writing this nearly 10 years after Berkshire Hathaway first bought into Apple, we now have the benefit of hindsight. So, did we nail our valuation estimates? Well … not really. In fact, despite our best efforts, we were badly wrong.

Using a conservative 20% annual growth rate, we estimated Apple's terminal value would be around $4.26 trillion in 2026. As at the time of writing (just six months shy of the 10-year anniversary of Buffett's investment), Apple's market capitalization is $2.92 trillion, a full $1.34 trillion below our estimate.

But this doesn't mean we made a mistake in our process. In fact, our valuation approach was sound. What it highlights is just how difficult it is to predict the future with precision. Valuation is not an exact science; it's an informed estimate. And that's exactly why the margin of safety is so critical. It's this single concept that separates Buffett (and those that think like him) from the countless mediocre "professional" investors of the world, who are trapped underperforming the market. It's the patience to wait for a margin of safety that ultimately gives us the long-term breathing room when the future doesn't go exactly as planned.

Buffett understood this. He had high conviction in Apple because the stock was trading far below even his most conservative estimate of intrinsic value. That deep discount drastically increased the probability of achieving his target return, and in the end, he did just that (and then some).

THE FOUR PILLARS IN CONTEXT

And that brings us to the conclusion of the Warren Buffett stock selection strategy, a strategy built on four timeless pillars:

1. **Understand the business.**
2. **Look for a moat.**
3. **Assess the management.**
4. **Calculate intrinsic value with a margin of safety.**

Sure, there was a little math. But if you embrace the process and stay grounded in these four timeless principles, you just might find yourself on the path to extraordinary wealth. It worked for Warren Buffett, Charlie Munger, Li Lu, Seth Klarman, Mohnish Pabrai, Guy Spier, Bill Ackman, Phil Town, and it's now working for me and my friends. Now it's your turn.

Remember what Buffett once said: the vast majority of Berkshire Hathaway's success has come from just 12 investments he's held since 1965, Apple being one of them. If you play the long game, stay patient, and keep hunting for those rare, fat pitches, you only need to hit a few to change your life.

STEP 4

STAY THE COURSE

CHAPTER THIRTEEN

RULES FOR BUYING AND SELLING

At this point, congratulations are in order. Over the course of a few hundred pages, you've come a very long way. Not only have you properly prepared yourself to invest and learned the strategy that millions of investors use to build long-term wealth on autopilot, you've now also absorbed the entire method that has helped Warren Buffett (and many others) reach billionaire status. That is no small feat, and I can guarantee that you now know more about rational, long-term investing than 99% of the population.

While it might sound like an exaggeration, this knowledge truly does have the potential to change the course of your financial future. Over time it will have more impact than working extra hours, getting a promotion, or even receiving an inheritance. I've seen this method change my own life, and the lives of the people around me, but to unlock that potential, there's one final piece we need to discuss: how to actually put these strategies into action. In other words, the practical rules for buying and selling.

BROKERAGE ACCOUNTS

To invest in ETFs or publicly traded companies, you'll need a brokerage account. These days, there's no shortage of options, and you've likely seen ads for many of them: Robinhood, Fidelity, Charles Schwab, Interactive Brokers, E*TRADE, M1 Finance, and others. So how do you choose?

The truth is the platform you use matters far less than what you choose to invest in. A helpful analogy is buying a can of Coca-Cola. You can find Coca-Cola at a gas station, a supermarket like Walmart, a convenience store like 7-Eleven, or even a restaurant. In this analogy, the Coca-Cola represents the stock you want to buy, and the different stores are the brokers. Each one might have a different layout and customer experience, but at the end of the day, you're still getting the same Coke.

It's the same with brokerage platforms. Some offer fractional shares; others provide commission-free trading. Some come with detailed analysis tools, while others support more advanced services like options trading. But all of them let you buy and sell shares, which is what really matters. So don't overthink it. Waiting six months to invest while you shop around for the perfect broker will likely cost you more than just getting started with one that's "good-enough."

That said, there are still a few characteristics worth considering so you can make a well-informed decision. Let's take a closer look.

When choosing a broker to invest your money with, one of the first things you should check is whether they're properly regulated. In the United States, trustworthy brokers are registered with the Securities and Exchange Commission (SEC) and are members of the Financial Industry Regulatory Authority (FINRA). These organizations enforce strict standards designed to protect investors, ensure transparent operations, and hold brokers accountable for misconduct. You can verify a broker's registration and even check for complaints or disciplinary actions through FINRA's free BrokerCheck tool online (found at brokercheck.finra.org).

Beyond regulation, another key layer of protection is SIPC coverage. The Securities Investor Protection Corporation insures your account up to $500,000, including up to $250,000 in cash, in the unlikely event your brokerage firm fails. This doesn't protect you from market losses, but it does safeguard your assets if the broker itself collapses or loses customer funds. Many large brokers also go one step further by carrying additional private insurance (often through providers like Lloyd's of London) that extends your coverage beyond SIPC limits. While it's rare to need this level of protection, knowing it's there can offer peace of mind, especially as your portfolio grows.

A final but critical safeguard is how your assets are held behind the scenes. US brokerage firms must keep your investments separate from their own corporate funds by using what's known as the custodian model. This means your stocks and cash are held in custody, either by the broker itself (if qualified) or by a third-party clearing firm such as Apex Clearing or Pershing. This separation ensures that even if the broker goes out of business, your investments remain legally yours and cannot be used to pay the broker's debts. In other words, you're not handing over your money to the broker; you're simply using their platform to access and manage assets held in your name.

Table 13.1 shows how all these safeguards apply to some of the better known brokerage firms.

Another important topic when it comes to brokerage accounts is brokerage fees. These are the fees paid to the broker when you buy or sell securities, essentially the cost of using their platform and services. Ten years ago, it was common to pay $3 to $5 per trade. But over the

Table 13.1 A Comparison of Brokers

Brokerage Firm	SEC and FINRA Regulated	SIPC Member	Additional Insurance	Custodian Model
Fidelity	Yes	Yes	Yes (Lloyd's of London)	Acts as its own custodian
Charles Schwab	Yes	Yes	Yes (Lloyd's of London)	Acts as its own custodian
Vanguard	Yes	Yes	Yes	Acts as its own custodian
E*TRADE (Morgan Stanley)	Yes	Yes	Yes	Uses Morgan Stanley custodial services
TD Ameritrade	Yes	Yes	Yes (via Schwab post-merger)	Uses Schwab's custodial services
Merrill Edge	Yes	Yes	Yes	Uses Bank of America custodial services
Robinhood	Yes	Yes	Yes (excess SIPC coverage)	Uses its own clearing firm (Robinhood Securities)
Interactive Brokers	Yes	Yes	Yes	Acts as its own custodian
SoFi Invest	Yes	Yes	Yes	Uses Apex Clearing as custodian
M1 Finance	Yes	Yes	Yes	Uses Apex Clearing as custodian

Note: Table 13.1 is accurate as of the time of writing, but brokerage features and protections can change over time. It should not be relied upon as a substitute for current information. Before opening a brokerage account, be sure to conduct your own due diligence to confirm that the broker still meets your requirements and offers the protections outlined here.

past decade, we've seen the rise of zero-commission brokers like Robinhood, and today it's increasingly rare for brokers to charge a standard trading fee up front. But naturally, this raises the question: if they're not charging brokerage fees, how are they making money?

The answer is that modern brokers have simply shifted to making money behind the scenes. Here are the six main ways they do it:

- **Payment for Order Flow**
Brokers route your trade to a third-party market maker, who pays them a small fee for the order. This practice is legal and widespread in the United States, though it can occasionally result in slightly worse execution prices. Brokers like Robinhood and E*TRADE rely heavily on this model.

- **Interest on Uninvested Cash**
If your money is sitting idle in your account, it may be swept into a low-interest account or affiliated bank. The broker earns a higher rate on that cash than they pass on to you and keeps the difference.

- **Margin Lending**
If you borrow money to invest, your broker charges interest, often at high rates. This can be a major profit source for brokers, especially on large balances, which is why margin accounts are heavily promoted. Be cautious. Margin can quickly get investors into trouble. If you see aggressive advertising for margin lending, ignore it or consider a different broker. Borrowing to invest is not part of the Warren Buffett playbook.

- **Premium Subscriptions**
Many brokers now offer paid tiers, such as Robinhood Gold or M1 Finance's discontinued "M1 Plus." These subscriptions include extra features, faster transfers, or higher interest on cash balances.

- **Fund Provider Revenue Sharing**
Brokers may receive payments from mutual fund or ETF providers in exchange for promoting certain funds on their platform. These "kickbacks" are not always transparent, so it's worth keeping an eye on the investment products being recommended.

- **Securities Lending**
  Brokers can lend out the stocks you hold in your account to short sellers, earning fees in the process. You still own the shares, but the broker profits from lending them out.

While none of these revenue models are inherently bad, it's helpful to be aware of how your broker makes money. You don't need to worry about them on a daily basis, but understanding the business model can help you make more informed decisions, especially around trade execution quality, interest on idle cash, and potential biases in investment recommendations.

But with that said, while it's important to consider these factors, this isn't something to lose sleep over. One of the biggest traps new investors fall into is *analysis paralysis*, in other words, spending so much time comparing brokers that they delay investing altogether. I've seen this happen to friends who got caught up in the details, only to invest months later than planned, or not at all. And that's the worst outcome. My advice? Spend an hour or so exploring your options. Fidelity, Charles Schwab, and Vanguard are three of the largest and most trusted brokers in the United States and could be a place to start. Pick the one that suits you best and get going. And don't stress. If you later discover that another platform better fits your needs, you can always switch. What matters most is simply getting started.

THIRTEEN RULES FOR BUYING AND SELLING

Firstly, you have no idea how much satisfaction it gives me that Chapter 13 happens to line up with our 13 rules for buying and selling—I didn't plan that! But yes, now that you've opened your brokerage account, there's only one thing left to do: follow the 13 rules to put your investing strategy into action. As we covered in Chapter 5, *The New Money Strategy* follows a core and satellite approach, meaning we start by building a solid foundation of passive investments, and then, if you're comfortable, allocating 20% to 40% of your portfolio to finding Buffett-style bargains. This structure gives you the best of both worlds. You have a dependable base that quietly compounds your wealth in the background, while also giving yourself the chance to uncover rare multibagger opportunities that could seriously transform your financial future.

But how exactly should we approach buying and selling? What rules should we follow to stay disciplined and avoid costly mistakes? Let's break it down, starting with the core: passive investing.

Passive Investing

When it comes to passive investing, the rules for buying and selling are simple. Since this strategy is built on dollar-cost averaging, your job is to invest a consistent amount at regular intervals, regardless of what the market is doing. Of course, life will naturally bring ups and downs so you may need to tweak the amount you invest from time to time, but the key rule is that you continue to invest consistently over time. That's the nonnegotiable part of this strategy.

Remember, passive investing is one of the few areas in life where being average is exactly what you want. And in this case, to achieve average means you must continue to buy into the market regularly, through both the highs *and* the lows. That is why setting up automated contributions is so valuable. It removes emotion from the process and keeps your strategy on track, even when life gets busy.

And what about selling? The rule here is just as straightforward: *we do not sell*. We do not sell just because the market is falling. We do not sell because we think it is overheated. We do not try to time the market *at all*. The only time you should plan to sell your passive investments is when you hit those golden years of retirement. Outside of severe and unexpected financial hardship (which is hopefully what your emergency fund is for), your passive investments should be left alone. The best thing to do is set it and forget it. Treat it as a lifelong commitment.

To summarize, passive investing works best when you keep it simple and stay consistent. It is not about reacting to headlines or predicting the next crash. It is about committing to a long-term strategy that builds wealth quietly in the background. To keep yourself on track, here are the first three rules to follow:

Rule 1: Only invest an amount you can regularly commit to.

Rule 2: Buy on a consistent schedule, no matter what.

Rule 3: Treat passive investing as a lifelong commitment and don't be tempted to sell.

Follow these rules, and your passive core will keep doing its job: steadily compounding in the background while you focus your attention on the exciting (and more hands-on) satellite portion of your portfolio.

Active Investing

When it comes to finding Buffett-style bargains, we need to follow a few additional rules to both increase our chances of success and protect us from making costly mistakes. Since this approach is more involved than the simplicity of dollar-cost averaging, we'll take a little extra time to walk through each rule carefully, starting with the rules for buying.

Rule 4: Only invest in a business you can understand.

This rule should come as no surprise. Before buying into any business, you must understand what it does, how it makes money, and what factors will drive its value over time. If you can't explain the business clearly to yourself, you shouldn't own it.

Remember Warren Buffett's "too hard" pile. If a company is too complicated or confusing, simply pass. Yes, you may miss out on some big winners in hindsight, but you'll also avoid the far more painful scenario of owning a business that goes south and not knowing what to do about it.

Rule 5: Do not invest in a business that has no competitive advantage.

Again, this should also come as no surprise. Reality is that capitalism is relentless. Companies are always fighting to take market share, launch better products, and outperform their rivals. In this environment, a business without a clear competitive advantage is vulnerable, and so is your investment. Without something protecting the business from competition, there's little to stop its profits, market share, and ultimately its value from falling.

Rule 6: Do not invest in a company with a management team that lacks integrity or skill.

This rule can be one of the hardest to follow. Sometimes everything else looks great on paper, but there's something off about the people running the business. Maybe there's a history of questionable decisions. Maybe they're not being fully transparent with shareholders. Unfortunately, poor or dishonest management can destroy a company faster than almost anything else. No matter how strong the business looks, if the people in charge can't be trusted (or can't execute) you're better off staying away.

Rule 7: Never buy a business unless it's at a 30% margin of safety, or preferably more.

Maybe a 10% margin of safety seems good enough. Maybe paying the full intrinsic value feels justifiable. But that kind of thinking is a surefire way to get hurt over time. Remember, valuation is not a precise science. No matter how careful we are, we will be wrong from time to time because the future is impossible to predict with certainty.

That's why we *must* build in a margin of safety. It gives us room for error and protects us from the natural ups and downs of business and life. As Buffett has said, his real winners only come around about once every five years. Think back to Buffett's punch card analogy. If you only had 20 investments to make in your lifetime, you would choose very carefully. Ultimately, this combination of a high-quality business available at a steeply discounted price is the golden ticket that can truly snowball our wealth, but we must be patient and allow time for these rare opportunities to present.

Rule 8: Once you find a margin of safety, load up the truck.

It's surprising how many investors do all the research, identify a great business, spot the margin of safety, and then hesitate. Some choose to "wait and see," only for the opportunity to disappear. Others take action but invest such a small amount that it barely moves the needle.

This hesitation is something Warren Buffett has often pointed to as his single biggest mistake in investing. At the 2001 Berkshire Hathaway Annual Shareholder Meeting, he and Charlie Munger spoke candidly about this pattern of missed opportunity:

Charlie Munger:	The mistakes that have been most extreme in Berkshire's history are mistakes of omission. They don't show up on our figures. They show up in opportunity costs. In other words, we have opportunities, we almost do it, and in retrospect we can tell that we were very much mistaken not to do it … Warren, we have blown-
Warren Buffett:	Billions and billions and billions—I might as well say it.

Charlie Munger:	And we keep doing it.
Warren Buffett:	Some might say we're getting better at it [...] I might add that when we speak of errors of omission (of which we've had plenty)—and some very big ones—we don't mean "not buying some stock where a friend runs it" or "we know the name and it went from $1 to $100," that doesn't mean anything. We only regard errors as being things that are within our circle of competence. So, if someone knows how to make money in cocoa beans or they know how to make money in a software company and we miss that? That is not an error as far as we're concerned. What's an error is when it's something we understand—and we stand there and stare at it—and we don't do anything. Or worse yet—what really gets me—is when we do something very small with it. We do an eyedropper's worth of it when we could do it very big. Charlie refers to that elegantly: when I do that sort of thing is when "I'm sucking my thumb."

Personally, I've fallen into this trap too. Even when everything lines up, it's remarkable how often there's still a part of you that freezes. So, take it not just from Buffett and Munger, but from me as well: when you find a truly exceptional opportunity with a wide margin of safety, don't hesitate. That's the time to act boldly. When you get the perfect pitch, don't forget to swing.

Rule 9: Don't expect a company to tick every box.

This is always a tough one to accept because, in theory, we'd all love to find the perfect company. But the truth is, perfect businesses don't exist. While it's helpful to have checklists and rules, reality is messy. Every business is different. They operate in different industries, have different capital structures, and are run by people with different goals and incentives.

You'll never find a company that ticks every single box perfectly, and the ones that come close are usually priced for perfection. That makes sense. Wall Street is willing to pay up for the safest, most predictable businesses. So how do we deal with this?

It starts by recognizing the *four nonnegotiables:* you must understand the business, it must have a moat, the management must be capable and trustworthy, and the price must offer a margin of safety. Beyond that, as you dig deeper into each pillar, your judgment will become increasingly personal. There's no formula for the perfect investment. A company might pass two out of three moat tests. It might be a great business, but in a capital-intensive industry, thus it might carry slightly more debt than you'd expect. These things do happen, and that's why the principles in this book should be treated as a guide, not a rigid checklist. In the end, it comes down to your own understanding, your conviction, and your ability to act when others hesitate.

The previous six rules form the foundation of the Buffett approach when it comes to *buying* shares. But there's another equally important topic we haven't yet explored: when to *sell*.

While Buffett famously says his favorite holding period is "forever," the reality is that not every investment will turn out to be the perfect long-term compounder you hoped for. Circumstances change. Sometimes the business improves; sometimes it deteriorates. So, it's important to know when it makes sense to step away.

With that in mind, here are the key rules to consider when deciding whether it's time to sell an investment.

Rule 10: If a business turns rotten, sell it.

Even the best businesses can lose their way. Management might change, the moat might erode, or the company might shift into an area you no longer understand. When the original reason you bought the business no longer holds true, it's time to reassess. Holding onto a declining company out of hope or stubbornness can be far more costly than admitting the investment no longer fits your strategy. Buffett himself has said that the most important thing to do when you're in a hole is to stop digging. If the facts have changed, don't be afraid to move on.

Rule 11: If the business changes, it's okay to leave.

No business stays exactly the same forever. Companies evolve. They might pivot into a new product line, shift their strategy, bring in new leadership, take on more debt, or enter industries that carry unfamiliar risks. Sometimes these changes are positive. But other times, they push the business outside your circle of competence or erode the qualities that made it attractive to you in the first place.

When that happens, it's okay to leave. Just because a company served you well in the past doesn't mean it deserves a permanent place in your portfolio. As Buffett says, "The stock doesn't know you own it." Holding on simply because it's been a long-term winner is not always a good reason to stay, especially if the business no longer fits your original investment thesis.

Rule 12: If an investment rises well beyond its fair value, don't be afraid to lock in a profit.

There is a classic value investing principle that says you buy a stock below its intrinsic value, enjoy the ride up, and sell once the price reaches fair value. That is the textbook approach to value investing, and it has worked well for many investors. Plenty of successful track records have been built on the back of disciplined buying and selling, recycling capital from fully valued businesses into fresh opportunities.

It is important to remember that a realized profit is still a profit. No one can take that away from you. Selling when a stock has exceeded your valuation is not a failure; it is a rational decision. After all, there is a risk in holding on for too long, hoping for more, only to see gains disappear.

So, if the business has clearly run well ahead of your estimate of value, it is entirely reasonable to sell. That is not impatience. That is discipline, and it keeps you grounded in your process.

But …

Rule 13: If a great business stays great, it's also okay to hold.

With that said, Warren Buffett has also shown that not all investments need to be sold just because they have reached or exceeded their estimated value. In recent years, he has become far more willing to hold outstanding businesses for the long term even if their price runs hot. His investment in Apple is the most well-known example. While it is no longer the value opportunity it once was, Buffett continues to hold because the business remains exceptional. It still has a strong moat, excellent management, and consistent growth.

The same can be said for a more speculative investment I made in Tesla back in 2017. Had I taken my early profit, I would have missed out on the extraordinary bull run in 2020 and 2021, when the stock surged from $32 to $407. That experience taught me that sometimes, the opportunity cost of selling a good business is higher than simply continuing to hold it.

The reality is, some companies have the rare ability to compound value for years, even decades. And the longer that runway, the more painful an early exit can be. As Peter Lynch famously warned, "Don't cut the flowers and water the weeds." A few high-quality compounders often account for the bulk of long-term returns, so the decision to sell should never be taken lightly.

So, what is the right decision? It depends. If the business is still strong, you understand it well, and you believe in its future runway, then holding may be the right choice, even if the valuation feels stretched. But if the fundamentals have weakened, or the price has run too far ahead of reality, taking profits may be the smarter move.

The key is to remain honest with yourself. Understand why you are holding, stay within your circle of competence, and be prepared to act if the facts change.

FOLLOW THE RULES

While I maintain that this book should serve as a guide rather than a rigid prescription, following these rules will go a long way toward keeping you out of trouble. And that's really what long-term investing is about. After all, Warren Buffett's famous Rule 1 is simple: "Don't lose money." Long-term investing is as much about protecting the downside as it is about capturing the upside. And the principles you've just read, combined with the broader foundation laid throughout this book, are designed to do exactly that.

As Buffett's mentor, Benjamin Graham, once put it:

> An investment operation is one which, upon thorough analysis, promises **safety of principal** [emphasis added] and an adequate return.

These rules may not be flashy. They're not about chasing the hottest stock or timing the perfect entry. But they are the exact same filters used by some of the greatest investors in history—Warren Buffett, Charlie Munger, Seth Klarman, Li Lu, Bill Ackman, Mohnish Pabrai, Guy Spier, and many more—to stay rational, focused, and disciplined.

So, feel free to dog-ear these pages. Highlight them. Rip them out and stick them on your wall if you need to. Investing success doesn't come from brilliance; it comes from staying rational, from sticking to your process. And it comes from having the humility to follow simple rules that help you keep your emotions in check and your capital intact.

As you move forward, let these rules serve as a compass. They won't guarantee success, but they'll help you avoid the most common (and costly) mistakes. And that, in the long run, makes all the difference.

CHAPTER FOURTEEN

STAYING ON TOP OF YOUR PORTFOLIO

At the start of this book, I promised you a simple plan for building lasting wealth, grounded in the wisdom of the world's greatest investor, Warren Buffett. Now, a few hundred pages later, you have that plan in your hands. And hopefully, you also have the confidence and mindset to put it into practice for the long haul.

Buffett-style investing is not complicated. The rules are clear, and the framework has stood the test of time. But while it is simple, it is not easy. If it were, everyone would be a billionaire like Warren.

So why aren't they? As we discussed earlier, most people do not fail at investing because of a lack of intelligence. They fail because of a lack of temperament. Millions have studied Buffett's approach, but most either never act or abandon the plan when emotions get in the way. That might be Buffett's most important lesson of all: discipline matters more than brilliance.

Even Warren Buffett has made mistakes. He has underperformed at times. But he *never* walked away from his strategy. He stayed the course. And that simple fact is the real reason why he is worth more than $160 billion today.

The same principle applies to you. None of what you have learned in this book will matter unless you act on it and stay committed. Building wealth is not a one-time decision. It is a long-term process that rewards patience and consistency.

In this final chapter, we will focus on five steps to help you stay on top of your portfolio, how to set up systems that quietly work in the background, and how to make sure the strategies you have learned do not just sound good in theory, but actually take shape in your real life.

GET THE SETUP RIGHT

There's a saying in farming: "Well sown is half grown." The same principle applies to investing. If you take the time to set things up properly at the beginning, you dramatically increase your chances of sticking with the plan and seeing results over time.

Investing success is not just about picking the right stocks or timing the market. It is about creating a system that fits your life, a system that you can follow through with even when you're busy, tired, or tempted by market noise. A well-thought-out setup removes friction, reduces decision fatigue, and helps you stay committed through the ups and downs.

Start with the essentials:

Understand your financial position. Are you genuinely ready to invest? How much can you realistically set aside each week?

This is not a guess. It should come directly from your personal profit and loss analysis. Once your bills and essentials are covered, what is left over—and how much of that are you willing to consistently invest?

Define your passive investing plan. Write it down. How much are you investing? How often? What ETF are you buying? Clarity is key. The simpler the plan, the easier it will be to follow. And the easier it is to follow, the more likely you are to stick with it over time.

Eliminate barriers. Set up your automatic bank transfers. Activate your auto-invest plan with your broker. Schedule your quarterly portfolio check-ins. Get your passive investing system humming in the background. The goal is to make it harder to fall behind than to stay on track.

Set aside time for your active investing preparation. Block out one hour on a weekend to explore some potential high-quality businesses you might want to dig into further. Refer back to the exercise in Chapter 6. Identify companies within your circle of competence. Choose one you find interesting and commit to walking it through the four-part Buffett-style analysis. Do you understand the business? Does it have a durable competitive advantage? Is management talented and trustworthy? And is it trading at a margin of safety?

This stage might not feel thrilling, but it is essential. A small investment of time now can prevent a lot of pain later. The best investors are not the flashiest or the smartest; they are the most prepared.

You do not need a perfect setup to begin with, and remember, as Peter Lynch says, if you're hitting 6/10 you're still doing fine. Right now, you just need to start working through the system, because once your system is in place, your investing journey shifts from theory to habit. And over time, consistent habits are what produce exceptional results.

BUILD A SIMPLE CHECK-IN ROUTINE

Once you've made some investments and your system is set up and running, the next step is to establish a simple routine to stay on track. This doesn't mean constantly checking your portfolio. In fact, the general rule of thumb is the less often you look, the better. But having a regular check-in, ideally once every quarter, helps ensure you remain intentional and aligned with your long-term goals.

Quarterly is the ideal rhythm for a few reasons. It gives you enough time between reviews to avoid overreacting to short-term market movements, but it also aligns with company reporting seasons. Public companies release their earnings reports and hold investor calls every three months, and around this time you see a lot of moving and shaking in stock prices. So, it pays to review your portfolio at the same time. Not only are you ensuring you stay up to date with the latest information, but you could even spot a new opportunity around this time. Whether you're investing passively or actively, this schedule gives you a natural point to stop, reflect, and make small course corrections if needed.

If you're investing passively, your quarterly check-in should be quick and straightforward. The goal is not to make changes, but to confirm that everything is still aligned. Ask yourself: Is your asset allocation still suitable? Has your financial situation changed in a way that affects how much you can invest? Are there any adjustments to fees or changes to your broker that might require your attention? Nine times out of ten, the answer will be no, and that's exactly what you want. A passive investing system that requires little maintenance is working as it should.

If you're investing actively, your check-in will be a little more involved. This is the time to review how both your investments and the companies on your watchlist are performing. Look at the latest earnings report and listen to management's commentary on the quarterly calls. These will give you all the insight you need to stay updated with what's going on at the company. Has the business grown or struggled? Has the competitive advantage strengthened or weakened? Is the management team speaking openly about the challenges at hand? Are they still allocating capital effectively and staying true to the long-term vision? It's also a moment to consider the valuation. Are you comfortable with holding the stock at current levels? Has the price dropped to give you a buying opportunity? Most times, nothing will have changed enough to convince you to act, but that's okay too. After all, as Buffett says, great investing is lethargy, bordering on sloth.

Checking in with your investments quarterly also helps investors avoid one of the most common traps I see: mistaking a big unrealized gain for a finished job. The truth is, following this method, you'll probably bump into a reasonably large paper gain in the first few years. Now while it's awesome to see one of your Buffett-style investments take off, many investors will see that and think, "Well, that one's all good," and they will mentally check out. They stop listening to earnings calls. They skip quarterly updates. And then out of nowhere, a year later, the stock drops sharply and wipes out most of their gain.

Worse still, because they haven't been paying attention, when this drop inevitably occurs, they have no idea what's actually going on anymore. They're stuck guessing, unsure whether the business has genuinely deteriorated or if the market is just overreacting. That's a dangerous position to be in.

Staying involved through a regular check-in keeps you confident, informed, and ready to act when necessary. It's not about doing more. It's about never losing touch with the businesses you own.

PREPARE FOR MARKET TURMOIL

At some point, the market will drop, and when it does, it often feels like the world is ending. Prices fall fast, headlines scream panic, and your instincts will tell you to do something. But here's the truth: downturns are not an exception. They are a feature of long-term investing.

Corrections and crashes are a normal part of market behavior. In fact, the stock market is likely to fall by 10% multiple times per year, and by 20% or more roughly every five. We've seen it time and time again—Black Monday in 1987, the dot-com crash in the early 2000s, the global financial crisis in 2008, the COVID-19 panic in 2020. Each of these events sent markets plummeting. And each time, they recovered.

Understanding this history is important because it prepares you to act rationally when fear sets in. Panic is *extremely* contagious, especially when the news cycle is filled with doom and gloom. If you're not careful, you can get swept up in the emotion and make decisions that undo years of progress. That's why it's essential to have a plan for what you'll do when volatility hits, before it happens.

One of the most powerful things you can do on an ongoing basis is filtering out the daily headlines. They are written to grab attention, not to provide balanced insight. Instead of focusing on the noise, simply follow our previous step. Every three months, return to your long-term thesis. Has the business you own fundamentally changed? Has your passive investing strategy stopped working, or is it just facing temporary pressure? Most of the time, the right move is to do nothing.

But most importantly, the key to staying rational during a downturn is to set clear rules before the panic begins. You need a plan to fall back on when emotions are running high. For example, you might promise yourself, "I will not sell any core ETF holdings" or "If one of my active investments drops 30%, I will review the thesis thoroughly before making any decisions." These kinds of personal commitments and rules take emotion out of the equation. You are no longer reacting impulsively. You are following a process that was designed with a clear and rational mindset.

Market downturns are never easy. But they are where long-term investors earn their edge. If you can stay calm while others panic, and even buy while others sell, you not only avoid unnecessary losses, you also give yourself the chance to benefit from the opportunities that often emerge when others are heading for the exits.

RECOMMIT TO THE STRATEGY EACH YEAR

Beyond your quarterly check-ins, it's important to pause once a year and step back. Take a moment to check in, not just on your portfolio, but on yourself.

At least once a year, sit down and review your investing strategy from the top. Are you still on track toward your financial goals? Are you contributing as much as you planned to? Has anything changed in your income, expenses, or family situation that might affect how much you can invest or how much risk you can take on?

This is also the time to realign your strategy with your time horizon. Are you still investing for the next 10, 20, or 30 years? Or are you getting closer to needing access to your capital? Your asset allocation, contribution rate, and even your investment style might evolve slightly as your life circumstances change. That is normal. The goal is not to keep everything rigid, but to make sure it continues to serve your long-term plan.

One helpful way to stay motivated through this annual process is to reflect on your progress. Look back at where you were a year ago. Review how much you've contributed, how your investments have performed, and what you've learned along the way. You might choose to jot down a few notes in a journal, update a personal milestone tracker, or simply reflect on how much closer you are to financial freedom.

Finally, zoom out. Revisit the big picture. Remind yourself why you are doing this in the first place. Is it to achieve financial independence? To give you, your partner, or your children a better life? To buy back your time? Anchoring yourself to that bigger goal helps you stay emotionally committed through the inevitable ups and downs of the market.

Recommitting once a year is not about changing your strategy. It is about reaffirming it. And that small act of reflection can give you the clarity and conviction you need to keep moving forward for another 12 months, consistently, and with purpose.

STAY DISCIPLINED AND STICK TO THE PLAN

If there's one truth that holds firm across every style of investing (passive or active), it's this: the biggest rewards go to those who stay the course. Time in the market beats timing the market. Always has. Always will.

You can have the smartest strategy, the best insights, and the perfect watchlist. But if you don't give your investments time to work, none of it matters. Compound interest only works if you let it. It needs years, even decades, to do the heavy lifting.

To see just how powerful this is, let's look at two examples.

First, take a passive investor who commits to investing $100 every week into a low-cost, broad-based ETF. They automate the process and let it run in the background for 40 years. Assuming an average annual return of 10%, they finish with approximately $2.4 million. And they only contributed $208,000 of their own money to get there. No guesswork. No stock picking. Just consistent investing and the patience to let compounding do its job. See Figure 14.1.

Now let's look at a more active approach, Buffett-style investing layered on top of your passive foundation. Imagine you spend the first five years learning, researching, and saving and eventually, you find a company that ticks all the boxes. After five years of patience, you make a $10,000 investment. That investment compounds at 15% annually for the next 35 years. (See Figure 14.2.) Another five years pass, and you find a second opportunity. Again, you invest $10,000, and it compounds for the next 30 years. This pattern continues

Figure 14.1   Investing $100 per week over 40 years.

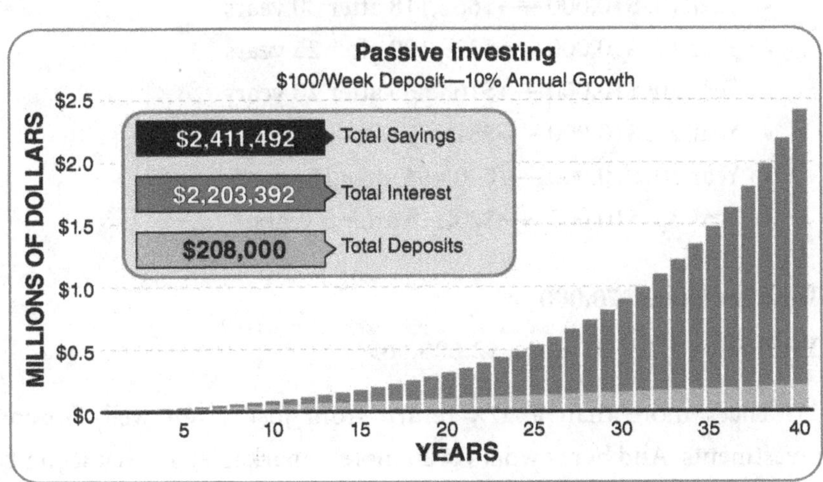

Figure 14.2 Buffett-style investing over 40 years.

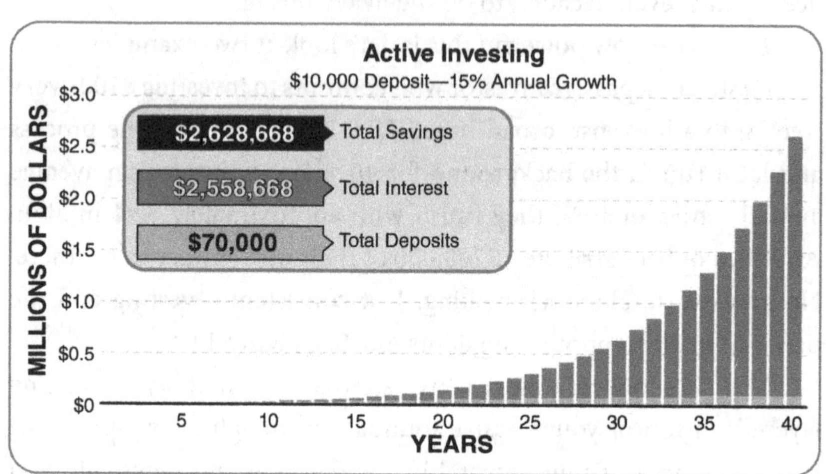

throughout your 40-year investing career. As Buffett himself has said, his best investment ideas have come around only once every five years or so.

Here's what that looks like over time, assuming each investment compounds at 15% annually:

- Year 5: $10,000 ⟶ $1,331,755 after 35 years
- Year 10: $10,000 ⟶ $662,118 after 30 years
- Year 15: $10,000 ⟶ $329,190 after 25 years
- Year 20: $10,000 ⟶ $163,665 after 20 years
- Year 25: $10,000 ⟶ $81,371 after 15 years
- Year 30: $10,000 ⟶ $40,456 after 10 years
- Year 35: $10,000 ⟶ $20,114 after 5 years

Total invested: $70,000

Total value after 40 years: $2,628,669

That's more than a 37× return from just seven well-chosen investments. And here's what's even more remarkable; if every second investment went to *zero*, you'd still walk away with over $1.7 million, or a 24× return on your capital.

Compare that to the passive strategy, where consistent compounding turned $208,000 into just $2.42 million. That's the power of concentrated, high-quality compounding and the discipline to let it play out over time.

The lesson is simple: regardless of your approach, your ability to stay invested is what drives the outcome. With compounding, the most lucrative years are always the ones at the end, so putting in the work now makes all the difference later. It's not about being brilliant. It's about being consistent. Markets will crash. Headlines will scare you. Results may stall for years. But those who stay calm, stay committed, and stay invested are the ones who ultimately win.

In the end, your future wealth depends far less on timing, talent, or luck and far more on discipline. Set your plan. Stick to it. And give it time to work.

START TODAY

That's really all there is to it. Simple, but not easy.

Becoming a great investor doesn't require complexity. Despite what Wall Street might have you believe, the tools you need are so straightforward they can fit inside a 60,000-word book. As Charlie Munger once said, the reason his and Buffett's approach hasn't spread more widely is precisely because it's so simple. And that remains true today.

But while the strategy is simple, the execution is not. Stick to your plan. Check in regularly. Stay rational when markets fall apart. That's the real challenge, and it's also my final message to you.

Right now, you have everything you need to transform your financial future. You've made the investment to learn. You've equipped yourself with the knowledge and the tools. But as you reach these final pages, you're facing the biggest risk of all: *inaction*.

Most people won't fail because they *didn't learn what to do*. They will fail because they never started.

Life will get busy. The kids need picking up. The power bill needs paying. Your favorite show just dropped a new season. It's all too easy to close this book and get swept back into the day-to-day.

So, my parting request to you is this: don't let that happen. Right now, before anything else, block out some time in your calendar over the next week and get started. Open a brokerage account. Automate your investments. Write down your checklist.

Don't let these lessons go to waste. Because as you've seen, this strategy has the power to build a small fortune over a lifetime. But only if you take that first step.

So, get that ball rolling. The future you want is within reach. I wish you all the best with your investing.

Many happy returns.

REFERENCES

Aladangady, A., Bricker, J., Chang, A., Goodman, S., Krimmel, J., Moore, K., Reber, S., Volz, A., and Windle, R. (2023). *Changes in US Family Finances from 2019 to 2022: Evidence from the Survey of Consumer Finances.* Board of Governors of the Federal Reserve System. Retrieved from https:// doi. org/10.17016/8799

Alphabet Inc. (2024). *Form 10-K: Annual Report for Fiscal Year Ended December 31, 2024.* Retrieved from https://abc.xyz/assets/77/51/9841ad 5c4fbe85b4440c47a4df8d/goog-10-k-2024.pdf

Apple Inc. (2015). *Form 10-K: Annual Report for Fiscal Year Ended September 26, 2015* [SEC filing]. US Securities and Exchange Commission. Retrieved from https://www.sec.gov/Archives/edgar/data/320193/000119312515356351/ d17062d10k.htm

Apple Inc. (2025). *Notice of 2025 Annual Meeting of Shareholders and Proxy Statement* [Proxy materials]. Retrieved from https://d18rn0p25nwr6d. cloudfront.net/CIK-0000320193/d5ac8341-3708-4b1d-89f5-6a0dcec45aa0. pdf

AT&T Inc. (2024). *2024 Annual Report.* Retrieved from https://investors.att. com/~/media/Files/A/ATT-IR-V2/financial-reports/annual-reports/2024/ complete-annual-report-2024.pdf

Auburn University. (n.d.). *Tyco International: Leadership Crisis (Case Study).* Harbert College, Auburn University. Retrieved from https://harbert.auburn. edu/binaries/documents/center-for-ethical-organizational-cultures/ cases/tyco.pdf

BlackRock/iShares. (2025). *iShares Core S&P 500 ETF (IVV)*. Retrieved from https://www.ishares.com/us/products/239726/ishares-core-sp-500-etf

BlackRock. (2025). *iShares US Healthcare ETF (IYH)*. Retrieved from https://www.blackrock.com/us/individual/products/239511/ishares-us-health care-etf

BNSF Railway. (2025). *BNSF Fact Sheet (March 2025)*. Retrieved from https://www.bnsf.com/bnsf-resources/pdf/about-bnsf/fact_sheet.pdf

Buffett, W. E. (1997). *Letter to Shareholders: Berkshire Hathaway Inc., 1996* [Annual letter]. Berkshire Hathaway. Retrieved from https://www.berkshire hathaway.com/letters/1996.html

Buffett, W. E. (1999). *Mr. Buffett on the Stock Market* [Excerpt/Report section]. Retrieved from https://www.berkshirehathaway.com/1999ar/ FortuneMagazine.pdf

Buffett, W. E. (2014). *Letter to Shareholders: Berkshire Hathaway Inc., 2013* [Annual letter]. Berkshire Hathaway. Retrieved from https://www.berkshire hathaway.com/letters/2013ltr.pdf

Buffett, W. E. (2017). *Letter to Shareholders: Berkshire Hathaway Inc., 2016* [Annual letter]. Berkshire Hathaway. Retrieved from https://www.berkshire hathaway.com/letters/2016ltr.pdf

Buffett, W. E. (2023). *Letter to Shareholders: Berkshire Hathaway Inc., 2022* [Annual letter]. Berkshire Hathaway. Retrieved from https://www.berkshire hathaway.com/letters/2022ltr.pdf

Cruise Market Watch. (2025). *Market Share: Worldwide Cruise Line Market Share 2025* [Online data]. Cruise Market Watch. Retrieved from https:// cruisemarketwatch.com/market-share/

Einhorn, N., Fisch, J. E., Gramitto Ricci, S. A., Le, M., and Sautter, C. (2023). *The Retail Investor Report*. Public.com. Retrieved from https://irlaw.umkc. edu/faculty_works/928/

Investopedia. (2025). *What Is the Average Annual Return of the S&P 500?* Retrieved from https://www.investopedia.com/ask/answers/042415/what-average-annual-return-sp-500.asp

Kerzérho, R. (2025). *The Passive vs. Active Fund Monitor: Year-end 2024* [Data Update]. PWL Capital, Inc. Retrieved from https://pwlcapital.com/ wp-content/uploads/2025/03/20250318-The-Passive-vs-Active-Fund-Monitor.pdf

Kochkodin, B. (2020). *US Airlines Spent 96% of Free Cash Flow on Buybacks* [News article]. Bloomberg. Retrieved from https://www.bloomberg.com/ news/articles/2020-03-16/u-s-airlines-spent-96-of-free-cash-flow-on-buybacks-chart

Lee, P. M. (2001). What's in a Name.com?: The effects of ".com" name changes on stock prices and trading activity. *Strategic Management Journal,* 22(8), 793–804. Wiley. https://www.jstor.org/stable/3094386

Massachusetts Securities Division. (2021). *Amended Administrative Complaint: In the Matter of Robinhood Financial, LLC, Docket No. E-2020-0047 (Massachusetts Uniform Securities Act Enforcement).* Commonwealth of Massachusetts, Office of the Secretary of the Commonwealth. Retrieved from https://www.sec.state.ma.us/divisions/securities/download/MSD-Robinhood-Amended-Complaint-Docket%20No-%20E-2020-0047.pdf

Meta Platforms, Inc. (2024). *Form 10-K: Annual Report for Fiscal Year Ended December 31, 2024* [SEC filing]. Retrieved from https://d18rn0p25nwr6d.cloudfront.net/CIK-0001326801/a8eb8302-b52c-4db5-964f-a2d796c05f4b.pdf

Public.com. (2023). *The Retail Investor Report.* Retrieved from https://public.com/research/2023-retail-investor-report

Robinhood Markets, Inc. (2021). *Robinhood Reports Second Quarter 2021 Results* [Press release]. Securities and Exchange Commission. Retrieved from https://www.sec.gov/Archives/edgar/data/1783879/000178387921000028/robinhoodexhibit991_6302021.htm

Robinhood Markets, Inc. (2022). *Robinhood Reports Fourth Quarter and Full Year 2021 Results* [Press release]. Securities and Exchange Commission. Retrieved from https://www.sec.gov/Archives/edgar/data/1783879/000178387922000022/robinhoodex991_12312021.htm

Royal Caribbean Cruises Ltd. (2020). *Form 10-K: Annual Report for Fiscal Year Ended December 31, 2019* [SEC filing]. Retrieved from http://app.quotemedia.com/data/downloadFiling?webmasterId=101533&ref=114824592&type=PDF&symbol=RCL&companyName=Royal+Caribbean+Cruises+Ltd.&formType=10-K&dateFiled=2020-02-25&CK=884887

S&P Dow Jones Indices. (2025). *SPIVA: S&P Indices versus Active* [Research report]. S&P Global. Retrieved from https://www.spglobal.com/spdji/en/research-insights/spiva/

Seeking Alpha. (2025a). *Berkshire Hathaway (BRK.B) Cash Flow Statement.* Retrieved from https://seekingalpha.com/symbol/BRK.B/cash-flow-statement

Seeking Alpha. (2025b). *Microsoft (MSFT) Income Statement.* Retrieved from https://seekingalpha.com/symbol/MSFT/income-statement

SlickCharts. (2025). *S&P 500 Companies by Weight.* Retrieved from https://www.slickcharts.com/sp500

StatCounter Global Stats. (2025). *Search Engine Market Share Worldwide.* Retrieved from https://gs.statcounter.com/search-engine-market-share

State Street Global Advisors. (2025). *SPDR S&P 500 ETF Trust (SPY).* Retrieved from https://www.ssga.com/us/en/individual/capabilities/spdr-core-equity-etfs/spy-sp-500

Trading Economics. (2025a). *United States Consumer Price Index (CPI).* Retrieved from https://tradingeconomics.com/united-states/consumer-price-index-cpi

Trading Economics. (2025b). *United States Personal Savings Rate.* Retrieved from https://tradingeconomics.com/united-states/personal-savings

US Bureau of Labor Statistics. (2020). *Median Weekly Earnings of Full-time Workers Increased 4.0 Percent in 2019. The Economics Daily.* US Department of Labor. Retrieved from https://www.bls.gov/opub/ted/2020/median-weekly-earnings-of-full-time-workers-increased-4-point-0-percent-in-2019.htm

US Bureau of Labor Statistics. (2025). *Usual Weekly Earnings of Wage and Salary Workers Second Quarter 2025* [News release]. US Department of Labor. Retrieved from https://www.bls.gov/news.release/pdf/wkyeng.pdf

US Social Security Administration. (2025). *What Is the Average Monthly Benefit for a Retired Worker?* Frequently Asked Questions. Retrieved from https://www.ssa.gov/faqs/en/questions/KA-01903.html

UK House of Lords. (2013). *Ready for Ageing? Report of Session 2012–13 (Select Committee on Public Service and Demographic Change, HL Paper 140).* The Stationery Office Limited. Retrieved from https://publications.parliament.uk/pa/ld201213/ldselect/ldpublic/140/140.pdf

Vanguard. (2025). *VOO: Vanguard S&P 500 ETF.* Retrieved from https://investor.vanguard.com/investment-products/etfs/profile/voo

Walt Disney Company. (2025). *Annual Report 2024.* Retrieved from https://thewaltdisneycompany.com/app/uploads/2025/01/2024-Annual-Report.pdf

Walmart Inc. (2025). *Form 10-K: Annual Report for Fiscal Year Ended January 31, 2025* [SEC filing]. Retrieved from https://stock.walmart.com/sec-filings/all-sec-filings/content/0000104169-25-000021/wmt-20250131.htm

INDEX

BrokerCheck (continued)
    184–185, 187–188, 191–193, 197,
    203, 208–213, 215, 217, 219, 221,
    223–226, 229, 233, 235–243,
    245–247, 253–255
Buffett-style investing, 10, 31, 60, 88,
    93, 147, 151, 184, 191, 193, 209, 245,
    249, 253, 254*f*
Burlington Northern Santa Fe (BNSF),
    116, 127–128, 134
Business descriptions, 101, 103,
    159, 163
Buybacks, 166–167, 180, 184–190, 196,
    213, 215
BUZZ (VanEck Social Sentiment ETF),
    67–68

C
Call Her Daddy (podcast), 122
Capital efficiency moat test,
    143–149, 181
Capital expenditures, 212, 217
Capital intensive businesses, 105, 127,
    147, 187, 189, 192, 194, 240
Carnival, 127
Cash bonuses, 166, 168, 170, 172*f*
Cash flow statements, 212–213, 217
Cash from operations, 217
CEO compensation, 165–174
Certificates of Deposit, 7
Charles Schwab, 84, 230, 234
Check-ins, 248–251
Chief executive officers (CEOs),
    152–159, 174–182, 185, 188–189,
    195–196
Chief financial officers (CFOs), 152
Chief operations officers (COOs), 152
Chief technical officers (CTOs), 152
Circle of competence, 14, 95–97,
    99–100, 239, 241, 243, 247
CNBC, 42, 157
Coca-Cola, 61, 113–116, 184, 230
Coinbase, 67
Complexity, 74–75, 159, 255

Compound annual growth rate (CAGR)
    calculator, 213
Confirmation bias, 43. *See also* Bias
Corrections, 250
Cost advantage moats, 124–125, 134
Costco, 125
COVID-19 pandemic, 11, 32–33, 83,
    122, 187–188, 190, 250
Cruise industry, 102, 105, 127, 128*f*, 189
Cryptocurrency, 12, 41, 60, 67
Cunningham, Lawrence A., 10
Current ratio, 191, 193–195, 195*t*, 196

D
Debt, 21–35
Debt adjustments, 207–208
Debt management, 180, 189–191
Debt-to-equity ratio, 102*t*, 191–193
Delta, 187
Department of Justice (DOJ), 129
Dexter Shoe, 51
The Dhando Investor (Pabrai), 10
Direct-to-consumer businesses,
    105–106
Discord, 120
Discounted cash flow analysis (DCF),
    199, 200, 206, 206*t*, 212, 220, 220*t*,
    222, 224
Disney+, 96, 102, 104, 105, 109*f*, 122
Diversification, 9, 62–63, 65, 68–69, 72,
    74–75, 91
Dividends, 115, 180, 184–189, 196
Dollar-cost averaging, 78–85, 78*f*, 81*f*
Domino's Pizza, 125
Dot Com bubble, 115, 183, 250
Dow Jones Industrial Average, 61
Downturns, 52, 53, 187, 250–251

E
Earnings calls, 155–156, 165, 249
Earnings per share (EPS), 166–167
EBITDA, 168
EBT (expense by income before
    provision for income taxes), 145